Perspectives on Student Affairs in South Africa

Edited by McGlory Speckman and Martin Mandew

Foreword by Prof. Ahmed Bawa

Published in 2014 by African Minds
4 Eccleston Place, Somerset West 7130, South Africa
info@africanminds.org.za
www.africanminds.org.za

African Minds is a not-for-profit, open-access publisher. In line with our goal of developing and fostering access, openness and debate in the pursuit of growing and deepening the African knowledge base and an Africa-based creative commons, this publication forms part of our non-peer-reviewed list, the broad mission of which is to support the dissemination of knowledge from and in Africa relevant to addressing the social challenges that face the African continent.

Paperback ISBN 978-1-920677-44-2
ePub ISBN 978-1-920677-60-2
eBook ISBN 978-1-920677-64-0

(cc) 2014 McGlory Speckman and Martin Mandew (eds)

Orders
For orders from within South Africa:
Blue Weaver
PO Box 30370, Tokai 7966, Cape Town, South Africa
Email: orders@blueweaver.co.za

For orders from outside South Africa:
African Books Collective
PO Box 721, Oxford OX1 9EN, UK
orders@africanbookscollective.com
www.africanbookscollective.com

Design and lay-out
COMPRESS.dsl | www.compressdsl.com

The editors gratefully acknowledge the financial assistance of SAASSAP in the production and printing of this book.

Foreword

South African higher education has a historic role to play, a role that has been identified and accepted by all sectors in our society and by important global institutions such as UNESCO and the World Bank. It is a powerful role that produces both public and private goods. The production of high level graduates, the production of new knowledge, the development of critical, active participants in our democracy, addressing the many legacies of apartheid, these are all examples of the public goods produced by the sector. The very high correlation between higher education and employability of graduates and their earning power and so on are examples of the private goods produced. At the heart of this project are the continuing challenges of access and success – understanding how best to address the deeply fragmented preparation of our students for higher education. Their educational, social and emotional preparedness for higher education is always at the heart of the debate when we consider that the drop-out rate of students in the system is at about the 50 per cent level for the system as a whole. This is shockingly higher than in other university systems.

Student welfare and student development have to be at the heart of any student-centred system that begins to conceptualise itself around the needs of the students in our system. It is a basic foundational requirement for student success. If we fail to provide holistic support to our students we face the danger of creating a revolving door syndrome, re-creating apartheid graduate dynamics, developing graduates who are not active, creative participants in the economy, and so on. The point to emphasise is that specialists in the areas of student services and student development are fundamental to the proper functioning of universities – to develop and nurture student growth in and beyond the classroom context so that learning takes place that prepares students for their future roles as active participants and contributors to the development of the economy and the deepening of our democracy.

It is important to understand that the inequalities that are so pervasive in South Africa re-create themselves at our universities. And so do the deep ills of our society – the devastation of HIV/Aids, the spreading of a deepening drug culture, the deep economic inequalities and so on. It is the student services sector that is at the coalface (and cutting edge) in terms of these challenges. Experienced practitioners pick up a number of things that lecturers are often not alert to. Invariably, these reflect in a microcosmic context what individual members of the broader society are going through. Institutions of higher learning, whose mandate is partly to find solutions to societal problems, cannot step aside and watch the situation deteriorating further on the grounds that it is not of their creation but a wider societal problem. Problems manifest in different ways in each context and they also vary in degrees of severity.

The Department of Higher Education and Training began many new initiatives, all ostensibly to improve the quality of the student experience for students. The massive increase in the financial aid allocation from the treasury, the development of a process of engagement on transformation, the commissioning of a study on student accommodation are examples of the kinds of interventions that impact on the quality of student experience. These have drawn heavily on those individuals and teams that work in the student services, student development arenas.

At a time when universities such as Durban University of Technology have begun to focus much attention on the idea of student-centredness, it is a pleasure to note that this book touches on the key issues that provide for a holistic understanding of the student as a young human being. Some of the issues raised in it are contentious, some are challenging to understand, some even controversial. This is good. It gives the reader a chance to engage with these. It provides for a safe platform for debate and for wrestling with the issues that concern our students and the services we provide to them. As a body of senior student affairs/student development professionals, SAASSAP has done exactly what is expected of it, leading from the front. I trust that more of its members as well as those who report to them will follow suit.

It should be remembered that student development and student success occur as a result of deliberate, well-planned and carefully structured development programmes and support initiatives and activities on the part of those who have been entrusted with this responsibility at our higher education institutions. The nature and extent of student development and success depends largely on the measure to which student services practitioners critically reflect upon and consistently review the assumptions, content, delivery and appropriateness of student development programmes, support structures, services and initiatives. This process of critical reflection, examination and renewal needs to be rigorous, goal-oriented and theoretically informed. It must take serious cognisance of all factors, personal, structural, social, cultural, psychological, internal and external, that impact on student ability to develop and succeed. In the final analysis, the process must produce sound knowledge and propose solutions that are practical and implementable, contributing towards student development and success.

This publication marks a very important milestone in the generation and expansion of endogenous knowledge in the field of student affairs and student services. It is the beginning of a crucial process designed to facilitate a much needed dialogue in pursuit of a common and shared vision for student development and success within the context of South Africa. The issues that are critically examined in this book are important and they affect students as they progress through our higher education system. We need to make sure that students receive the necessary development, support and guidance to succeed. This publication is an important resource for our student affairs practitioners and I am happy to support the effort to bring to fruition the formation of a shared vision for student development and success.

Prof. Ahmed Bawa
Vice-chancellor, Durban University of Technology
and past president of Higher Education South Africa (HESA)

Preface

The creation of a single Department of Higher Education in 1994 has been a blessing for student affairs in South Africa. Unlike with the dilemma faced by the world-renowned South African liberation theologian Albert Nolan (1989) who was not sure whether the book he sat down to write was for one or two nations in one country; or president Thabo Mbeki (1999) who ten years later, found himself having to confront the problem of 'two nations' in one country, separated by economic statuses, many student affairs practitioners would attest to being one family occupying different rooms of the same home. They meet regularly at national bodies such as the South African Association of Senior Student Affairs Professionals (SAASSAP), the National Association of Student Development (NASDEV) or the offshoots of these structures such as the Association of College and University Housing Officers-International South Africa Chapter (ACUHO-I SAC), Financial Aid Practitioners of South Africa (FAPSA), Student Health, Sports, Women and Justice structures, etc.

In line with the ideals of a democratic country, these structures and sub-structures are not separated by affiliation to one or another racial group. Nor are they separated by ideological preferences but by their functions. If there are any discrepancies in practice, they are based on the bouquets different institutions can afford for their student support and development programmes. This is not said naively as we are all too conscious of the historical imbalances which have given some institutions a financial and material edge over others. However, we recognise the free access policies for all students who meet the requirements of various institutions.

It is therefore with a sense of pride that we present this volume to student affairs departments, our institutions of higher learning and local and international partners. We are confident that each of these, wherever they are located, will identify with an aspect or two of the lot that is presented in this volume. Although issues might be more pronounced in some institutions than in others, they are generally experienced across the board. We could go further to say that they all have an international dimension as well. Hence the utilisation of resources and solutions from international contexts.

We have consistently referred to this publication as a 'volume'. This is not arbitrary. It is indeed not a book in the sense of it having a storyline running through like a thread or chapters that are intended to hang together. It is a collection of papers from various authors with student affairs experience who express their views on various topics, from different perspectives. Hence *Perspectives on Student Affairs in South Africa.*

There are many student affairs topics to explore. Each is like a green-field as it presents new challenges and dynamics that have not previously existed. Yesterday's answers and approaches may therefore not necessarily be the most appropriate for today. Contemporary tactics and solutions have to be found. This obviously cannot be achieved through a volume or two of papers. It will take a lot more, including applying research protocols, evaluating and assessing, even using trial and error over time. Volumes of this nature can only introduce possibilities and pointers in particular directions.

This volume is therefore about these possibilities. At least nine active and former student affairs practitioners have expressed their views on selected topics. The advantage is that they are all South Africans although they have drawn a lot from the insights and best practice of other contexts. It is hoped that their contributions will inspire others to commit to a third, fourth and many more volumes to come. Boldness in taking the first step will demonstrate to others that this is doable.

It must be mentioned that this volume was primarily inspired by the sad realisation that since the creation of a single department of higher education, there has been little to no student affairs literature coming from South Africa. In 2002 Roger Ludeman, then Fullbright scholar in South Africa, was guest editor along with Cecil Bodibe the editor of the first and only issue of *Thuso*, the student affairs journal. The 2003 volume which was edited by Martin Mandew and a few uncoordinated papers published by individuals in non-student affairs journals since then, are the only literature currently available from South Africa. There may be a lot more in the pipeline as some practitioners have recently acquired qualifications in student affairs-related programmes while others are in the process of researching. Hopefully, the new *Journal of Student Affairs in Africa* which has a more continental outlook and contribution will create another platform for a sharing of ideas and for building the body of knowledge in the discipline on the African continent.

At a secondary level, the idea of putting together a publication of this nature was born out of a negative situation, namely, a failure to get enough papers to publish from the 2011 SAASSAP Conference under the theme of 'caring institutions' as envisaged by the 2010 Ministerial Summit on Transformation in Higher Education. Contributors to this volume were hand-picked around the middle of 2012 and they all cooperated. As editors we are grateful for the opportunity to lead this project. However, it is individual contributors who take accountability for the academic integrity of their papers. A sincere word of gratitude therefore goes to them, not only for their willingness to contribute but also for their patience in waiting for a volume that has been in the making for the past eighteen months. This is not unusual. However, this time around it is the fast-changing higher education environment that has made some topics slightly irrelevant, forcing an updating in both content and approach. Thanks to the publisher, African Minds, as well for their patience and understanding.

The Department of Higher Education and Training has enacted several policies and produced a number of guidelines on various issues affecting higher education recently. However, it is not the Department that is active on the ground but the student affairs practitioner. Equally, it is the student, guided by the practitioner, who will give effect to the policies and guidelines. The platform created by a Resources Series as we hope this project will become, should enable many to reflect on their praxis, share best practice and interpret policy for implementation.

A word of gratitude also goes to the individuals who at various stages have read parts of this volume or the entire draft. We are grateful to them for their insights and the critical questions they have raised. Those outside the SAASSAP family include Dr Roger Ludeman, a longtime friend of SAASSAP and President Emeritus of the International Association of Student Affairs, Prof Rob Midgley of the University of Zululand, Dr David Levy of the University of South Africa, Dr John Boughey of the University of Zululand and Mr Edwin Smith of the University of Pretoria. We would also like to thank SAASSAP for financial assistance.

The Editors
McGlory Speckman
Martin Mandew
March 2014

Biographical notes

Birgit Schreiber is a director of the Centre for Student Support Services and Counselling at the University of the Western Cape. She holds a PhD in educational psychology and is currently heading the research and development portfolio of SAASSAP.

Llewllyn MacMaster is former dean of students at the University of Stellenbosch and is currently project leader in the newly established Centre for Inclusivity at the same university. He holds a PhD in theology. He is a former secretary general of SAASSAP and is its current president.

Martin Mandew is a former assistant on student affairs to the vice-chancellor of ML Sultan Teknicon (now Durban University of Technology) and a former executive member of SAASSAP. He holds a PhD in theology and is currently director of the Midlands Centre of DUT in Pietermaritzburg.

Matete Madiba is currently the director of student affairs at the University of Pretoria. She holds a PhD in (educational) information systems with specialisation in curriculum development and student success. She is a former deputy director in the department of education innovation at the University of Pretoria.

Lullu Tshiwula is deputy vice-chancellor for student affairs at the University of the Western Cape. She holds a PhD in social work and is a professor in the department of social work.

Hanlé Kirkcaldy is a clinical psychologist in the student support division at the University of Pretoria. She holds an MA in clinical psychology, an MPhil in applied ethics, and has a keen interest in the area of ethics in counselling young people.

Zethu Mkhize is currently the acting dean of students and head of the Aids unit at the University of Zululand. She holds a PhD in social work and is a former lecturer at the University of Zululand.

McGlory Speckman is a former dean of students at the University of Pretoria and is currently on secondment at the University of Zululand as advisor to the vice-chancellor on student affairs. He holds a PhD in theology, is a professor in the faculty of theology at the University of Pretoria and is a former executive member of SAASSAP. He was responsible for the research and development portfolio on the SAASSAP Executive.

Introduction

There is a lacuna in the area of home-grown student affairs reading and published resources in South Africa. Apart from a volume that was commissioned by the Centre for Higher Education Transformation (CHET) as part of the Effective Governance project, and edited by Martin Mandew *et al.* (2003), there has been, to our knowledge, no other published resource in the last decade or so. The SAASSAP journal *Thuso* which was launched in 2003 was apparently stillborn. Even the South African Association for Senior Student affairs Professionals (SAASSAP) conference proceedings of the past sixteen years have hardly found their way to publishing houses.

Understandably, the South African higher education system has only been consolidated under one department since 1994. Prior to that there were practically three systems based on unequal racial differentiation which in effect produced different epistemologies with varying methodologies to Student affairs practice. The period between 1994 and today more or less coincides with the existence of SAASSAP (2001) and is, in effect, a time of making new beginnings. However, the past cannot be used as an excuse for a failure to reflect on best practice, if any, of the different systems that existed previously. Nor does it provide an exoneration from the obligation of documenting SAASSAP conference proceedings, which are crucial for the project of developing home-grown resources.

Failure to reflect on local best practice or produce new knowledge has opened up a huge gap for the proliferation of foreign, particularly American, models and theories. This is both a blessing and a curse. It is a blessing to the extent that the Student affairs practice in South Africa is plugged into an international community of professionals, a welcome platform for sharing as well as learning. Without the support and mentorship of our international partners and colleagues it would not have been possible for South African Student affairs practitioners to have made the strides they have in the last decade and a half.

On the other hand, it is also a drawback to the extent that it has unintentionally led to the paralysis of the creative spirit of South African practitioners. Sharing or contribution to the international community of professionals is overtaken by a tendency to imbibe in the name of learning. There is little original about the practice and philosophy of most professionals in student affairs – from the theory of student support and development to the philosophy of student housing, one finds the same imported jargon and literature. Most ideas are transported to the South African context without due consideration of different circumstances – a disservice, in our view, to our international partners who also wish to learn from South Africa. Is there no uniquely South African contribution to make – locally and internationally? Surely, contexts are different and effective solutions to challenges, although similar, are those that are informed by the local contexts (Coetzee 1989).

This volume does not pretend to provide an alternative to the present state of affairs. However, it is intended to provide space for local practitioners to begin reflecting on their local practice and experience in light of available theories and models. Although it is slightly different from the previous publication in both its content and approach, it is intended to build on the foundation laid by it. A multi-subject approach has been preferred with the full knowledge that each topic can be a theme on its own. The idea is to get people to think about the various issues raised and the perspectives from which they have been raised so as to prepare them for subsequent contributions in specific thematic volumes. In other words, it is intended to be a springboard for future work in this SAASSAP resource series.

There are many grey and challenging areas in our context. Yet these areas are crucial for the development of student affairs in South Africa. It is worth mentioning some of those that need urgent attention. The area of student governance, for example, is crucial for the stability of higher education institutions. Besides student affairs in general being central to the life of an institution, student governance in particular needs special attention. No serious reflection has on a philosophical and conceptual level to date taken place on its definition, the value it is intended to add to the lives of students, its enhancement of the core business and culture of the institution and its relationship to the external stakeholders, if at all it should be linked externally. Generally, student governance has tended to be narrowly defined as the student representative council (SRC) to the exclusion of all other student governance structures and substructures that form the broad base. Different views on this need to be documented as we work towards a common understanding.

Historically black institutions (HBIs) in particular can make a valuable contribution in this regard. They were forced by historical circumstances to serve as bastions of resistance to apartheid and hubs of political activism. These accolades have followed them from the era of apartheid to the democratic dispensation. Many of the leaders at the reins of South African government are products of such institutions. In that sense, they undoubtedly have a very rich history.

At first glance it would appear that our post-1994 crop of student leaders have not been able to make a transition from resistance to celebration and development, as they continue to operate in a combative mode during what should be an era of reconstruction. Their models are heroes of the struggle against apartheid. Any digression from the anti-apartheid forms of engagement is seen as a betrayal of a 'struggle'. With the exception of an attempt by JJ Tabane *et al.* (2003), which controversially places student governance on the same equation as university council on governance and even refers to 'cooperative governance', there has been no critical reflection on, or explication of, the role of student governance in an institution of higher learning in a context where the country is struggling to get to grips with the notion of democracy at both a philosophical and practical level. Not surprisingly, student governance is seen as a site of ideological struggles between contending political affiliations, often leaving little space for grooming leaders for the future of the country.

Perhaps, as student affairs practitioners, we should not be surprised by the combative stance of many of the student governance leaders. We are aware of a plethora of problems and challenges that students continue to face and contend with. We are aware that the problem of hunger is faced by thousands of students on a daily basis; the problem of student accommodation forces many students into a life of squalor as they become virtual squatters in the grime and crime-ridden parts of our towns and cities; the issue of poverty means that many students share their already inadequate financial aid grant with their impoverished families; and academic and financial exclusions cast students into the world of the unemployed and dependency, indebted to NSFAS. In a sense we should not be surprised that the 'struggle' continues unabated.

In line with the school of thought which advocates that effective solutions come from the local context (Korten 1990), it is our view that the solution to the above challenges requires a constructive multi-pronged strategy by all concerned, viz. leadership, student affairs leaders, higher education leadership and the state. However, two things need to happen: first, benchmarking in successful democracies has to take place. South Africans seem unable and unwilling to separate a student agenda from the national party-political agendas. Perhaps we all need to learn from other contexts that it is possible to do so without neglecting the incubatory role. Secondly, a Student affairs catalyst is necessary. Currently, everyone, Student affairs practitioners included, seems to be flowing with the stream that uncritically follows the initial model that is fraught with challenges and glaring shortcomings. The dominant model is fashioned on the South African parliament and its various arms, but it has proved difficult to manage and develop into a proper democracy at the level of student governance. In some instances students not affiliated to organisations are excluded and effectively disenfranchised while others from opposing political parties are often marginalised by the group that is in power, resulting in a counter-productive fragmentation of the student body and unhealthy tensions. Hence the need for a catalyst who will force all involved to pause and think. A challenge to reflect on this issue is in fact a call to practitioners to rethink their own practice while also facilitating a mindshift among the students. They are a crucial component of a turnaround strategy.

Another theme that has not been addressed adequately over the years is student development. The better-resourced universities seem to be doing much better than their not so well-resourced counterparts. However, it is a question of each being for itself. Ludeman *et al.* suggest that student affairs has gone through three phases, viz, the 'parenting phase', the 'student development phase' and 'integrated support phase'. The last of these three is a very recent development. South Africans seem to have understood the latter part of the middle phase which started in the 1960s. Elsewhere in the world, our counterparts have been grappling for almost a decade and a half with issues of integrated student support. It is only very recently that South African universities have begun to look for teaching and learning vice-principals / deputy vice-chancellors, to address the issue from that angle. We are not optimistic about the outcome as it is still going to result in the same dichotomy between what the Americans refer to as 'college' and 'faculty'. College in this case refers more to learning and development outside the classroom than to an institution. The champion of a holistic student development and integrated learning in the American context seems to be student affairs, not the teaching and learning portfolio, although there are strong collaborations based on student learning outcomes.

It is for this reason that the theme of the SAASSAP conference of 2012 focused on a 'student's developmental pathway'. A clear pathway, from orientation to graduation, must be articulated. This will enable all role-players to see where they fit into the scheme and contribute in ways that add value and make a difference. While there is a line between academic development and social and personal development, it should be realised that the line is very thin. One does not happen effectively without the other. Students have 'one head, one heart' and learning occurs holistically, not in bits and pieces. The theme of the SAASSAP conference was intended to highlight this approach as well as to make the point that student affairs cannot be a mere partner but an actively involved and leading one if the model is to succeed. Others have taken the initiative because student affairs has not risen to the occasion. If this introduction could play a catalytic role in initiating a volume on this theme, its aim would have been achieved.

Counselling has been with student affairs since its early days. Yet it continues to pose challenges. It is in fact, a good example of the problem this volume is attempting to address. A lack of home-grown resources often makes it difficult for counsellors to strike the right chord. Some counsellors have confessed during conferences that the international literature used during their training has at times failed them when they needed it the most. Some theories worked better than others. But what could be better and more effective than home-grown theories informed by the local context? This may not lie in the Student affairs domain, but Student affairs should have an input in research conducted by academics in this area.

Human behaviour is often influenced by the material conditions in a given environment. Hence it is difficult to attach a universal application to every theory. It may well be, for example, that the background of broken homes is common in all contexts, but an individual's threshold in a given context might be influenced more by his/her grooming in that context than universal human behaviour. There may be developmental problems for all young people at a particular age. But the reaction of an individual will largely reflect his/her background.

Another area of concern since the establishment of SAASSAP has been the lack of a Student affairs methodology. This appears to be a universal concern. However, not much has been done about it, since student affairs is comfortably accommodated by disciplines such as psychology and education. Many writers, including a couple in this volume, have been lamenting the absence of a methodology without reflecting on possibilities. The new thrust in the direction of a qualification is also located in Education and there is no sign from what we have seen that a Student affairs methodology is in the making. Elements of a possible student affairs methodology have been emerging over the years. They include the following:

i) *Support:* emotional, material, academic
ii) *Learning experience:* formal, informal, recognition of social capital
iii) *Development:* leadership, personal, shared values
iv) *Wellness:* mental and spiritual, physical
v) *Social responsibility:* volunteerism, citizenship, participation, academic service learning

Student affairs researchers have to focus on this as a priority as well as finding ways to assist practitioners to communicate to key stakeholders, internal and external academy what it is that comprises student affairs as a field and how that intertwines with, and contributes to, carrying out of institutional mission and successful student learning outcomes.

This volume has eight papers grouped under three themes: overview of issues and challenges; access, support and success; and holistic support for students. The theme on leadership has been shifted to a subsequent volume where it will be fully developed. We have elected to stick with the language of 'papers' rather than 'chapters' so as to avoid raising expectations about coherency, uniformity and methodology. These remain individual perspectives on various topics. The volume is only intended to be a springboard. It creates a platform for individuals to present their perspectives on the various issues with which student affairs in South Africa is grappling. The papers may not all be of the same length, but we have allowed for a digression from the 15-page limit where a topic is pioneering and needs substantial elaboration. In pursuit of an integrated approach to student success and development, we have also allowed papers with a teaching and learning thrust.

Following this introduction is the first paper, which provides an overview of key challenges of Student affairs at an international level. Birgit Schreiber is grappling with changing trends in the international arena. These include globalisation, internationalisation, professionalism and the need for a normative meta-framework for South Africa. Student affairs in South Africa has for too long been out of the loop as a result of the international cultural boycott. While it is engaged in the internal process of reconstructing itself it also has a lot of catching up to do.

A sister paper to this follows with an overview of the same at a local level. The paper is presented by Llewellyn MacMaster. Drawing from both national challenges and their international parallels, Llewellyn zooms in on issues that affect student affairs professionals at an institutional level. The paper is located within the framework of the National Plan of the department of higher education and training. He cautions student affairs professionals against marginalising themselves by not embracing an integrated approach.

Martin Mandew, pursuing the integrated approach to student support as already alluded to by MacMaster, presents the first paper with a teaching and learning focus. He traces the difficult history and struggle of academic development as a field with the view to highlighting the original agenda and intention of academic development and its subsequent maturation as a discipline in its own right. He argues that student affairs as a field can learn from and also work collaboratively with academic development for the benefit of the student.

Mandew's paper is followed by a paper by Matete Madiba on student success and structural inequality. Madiba looks at the notion of integrated student support as well as the meaning of 'graduatedness' in the broader context of student success. She calls for a coalition between the academy and organised formations from without in pursuit of the objective of student success.

Completing the trilogy on the teaching and learning thrust, Lullu Tshiwula and Ncedikaya Magopeni explore factors that impact negatively on access to university by students from rural and disadvantaged areas from the perspective of two diverse groups of respondents they investigated. They present the respondents with recommendations on how the challenges of access can be mitigated.

The volume changes gear to three papers which approach support from three angles. For lack of a better term, we have classified them under holistic support. Hanle Kirckaldy's paper on counselling deals with ethical issues and the obligation of counsellors to the young people they are working with on the one hand, and the institutions of higher learning who are their employers on the other. It concludes that there are instances in which the counsellor may use discretion and reveal to a third party without necessarily behaving unethically.

Zethu Mkhize reflects on the place of social work in institutions of higher learning. She traces its historical role as advocated by older and more experienced scholars of the discipline and its glaring absence historically in higher education institutions. Making the case for its place in student affairs, she posits the various roles the social worker is called to play in supporting students, thereby contributing to their development and success.

A third and final paper deals with material support models available to students. It argues that the current interventions in higher education amount to deficit-based approaches which create ground conducive to the development of clienthood with its baggage of paternalism, dependency and entitlement. The paper asserts that the aim of all assistance should be to facilitate success and create citizenship. It suggests that an asset-based approach is the solution to the problem.

The Editors

Key challenges facing student affairs: An international perspective

Birgit Schreiber
University of the Western Cape

Summary

This paper attempts to describe student affairs in the developed and the developing world[1], to review some of the challenges and opportunities emerging from globalisation and internationalisation, and to describe the trend of professionalisation which has swept over international student affairs since the benchmark was set by the USA. The paper concludes with a key lesson learnt from the international perspective, which is the urgent need in South Africa to develop a normative meta-framework, based on theory and grounded in the fluid reality of higher education in South Africa.

Introduction

Even before the liberation of 1994, South African universities had entered the international community of higher education. The dramatic changes in the global arena have significantly impacted on South African higher education, on its organisational structures, its models and frameworks, its curricula and pedagogic approaches, its discourses and its conceptualisation of, and responsiveness to, community. The changes, internationally and nationally, have challenged higher education's historically dualistic notions around student affairs, and has compelled an engagement with pluralist constructions of our reality, and in the process called into question higher education's very *raison d'être* (Buroway 2010; Hirt 2006).

Being part of a global consciousness promotes a shared understanding of the complexities of equality, human rights and social justice (Nussbaum 1995). Gunderson (2005) argues that internationalisation is 'at the heart of liberal education', which promotes a global consciousness and is a key concern for student affairs nationally and internationally (Gunderson 2005: 246). South Africa, much like other countries, 'now partakes, albeit unequally, both in the local and the global' (Cloete & Muller, 1998: 19), and hence, understanding ourselves within the context of internationalisation and globalisation is imperative for South African Student affairs, not only to benefit from a shared system of ethics, but also to contribute towards this global consciousness.

It is essential that student affairs is familiar with international trends, shifts and policies and other events which occur in the macro context and might impact on higher education and student affairs. An example which illustrates the importance of this is the UNESCO World Conference on Higher Education: Vision and Action in 1998, which culminated in a declaration directly related to the domain of student affairs (UNESCO 1998). Another example is the Bologna Process in Europe which had implications for internationalisation of student affairs (Urbanski 2009). Yet another is the Dearing Report, which initiated performance-related funding in England and impacted on monitoring and evaluation practices across Europe (UKCISA 1999). Perhaps the Spelling Commission in the USA was one of the most important events in the international student affairs landscape. It demanded clear accountability measures in student affairs in the USA and this new development significantly influenced the international benchmark (USDE 2006).

International shifts do not only affect pragmatic issues but also discourses, constructions of reality and epistemologies. This shift towards pluralist epistemologies emerges from the increase in diversity of heterogeneous student populations, from the internationalised campus realities impacting on culture and processes, and the national as well as global commitment to massification and transformation of higher education. Student affairs needs to embrace these emerging fluid and pluralist *weltanschauungen* which result from being part of a global international education context[2].

Harper (1996) and Mandew (2003), in reviewing South African student services, present some key challenges for South African student affairs, and this paper on the international perspective aims to engage with some of these challenges. To this end, the international perspectives presented in this paper attempt to describe student affairs in the developed and the developing world[3], to review some of the challenges and opportunities emerging from globalisation and internationalisation, and to describe the trend of professionalisation which has swept over international student affairs since the benchmark was set by the USA. The paper concludes with a key lesson learnt from the international perspective, which is the urgent need in South Africa to develop a normative meta-framework, based on theory and grounded in the fluid reality of higher education in South Africa.

Student affairs in South Africa 'has at very critical and [...] opportune moments not always risen to the challenges of change' (Mandew 2003: 1). Through reviewing formative influences in the macro context this paper aims to galvanise the national student affairs community towards engaging with these 'challenges of change'[4].

Understanding student affairs in developed and developing regions

Higher education institutions worldwide are under pressure to address issues related to massification, such as access and equity, quality assurance and standardisations (Dalton 1999; Gupta 2006; Pascarella & Terenzini 2005; UNESCO 1998). Issues of efficiency, of student success and of employability beyond graduation are crucial concerns for student affairs worldwide (Gupta 2006; UNESCO 2004). These issues affect the developed and the developing world, albeit in different ways, and student affairs is uniquely positioned to contribute towards the engagement with these issues.

The International Association of Student Affairs and Services (IASAS) describes the aim of student affairs as follows: 'to assist students in navigating their journey through the tertiary education landscape and add to their repertoire of educational and lifetime learning experiences'[5]. Moreover, enabling epistemological access to higher education discourses and facilitating qualitative changes in cognitive and affective development remains a central concern of student affairs.

IASAS, although dominated by Western presence and participation, has acknowledged the tension between the 'developed' and the 'developing' student affairs and cautions that perhaps there has been a rush to 'adopt/adapt Western forms of higher education, sometimes without regard for the cultural appropriateness of these models'[6]. Challenges emerge when engaging with the 'developed' countries which have 'professional' student affairs domains, from a 'non-professional' position within a 'developing' country such as South Africa.

Each region has challenges and each region emerges with different solutions to its local context and its relationship to the global arena.

Student affairs in developed regions

Student affairs has a long history, emerging primarily from the universities of the UK and the USA. Although the higher education institutions in the USA, Australia, the UK and the European continent have historically fairly different constellations and structures, the emerging student affairs models and practices are beginning to look rather similar (Buroway 2010; ESU 2008; ISAP 2009; Sidhu 2006; Singh, Kenway & Apple 2005; Urbanski 2009).

The different historical trajectories of higher education are important for an understanding of student affairs and are described by Du Toit (2007), who identifies the Anglo-Saxon, the Continental-Roman (strongly influenced by the German tradition), and the Anglo-American models of higher education. In essence, the Continental-Roman model is centrally managed by state bureaucracies[7]. The Anglo-Saxon model, which later informed the Anglo-American, is premised on strong faculty association and 'rather than expressing the rational order of the public sector or the administrative state, universities were rooted in local communities, served regional needs, and reflected local communal identities' (Du Toit 2007: 54). These models form the basis to higher education in which student affairs is embedded in different ways. This is illustrated in the section below, which describes the emergence of student affairs within these models in various developed countries.

United States of America, Australia and the UK

In the USA, the student affairs divisions emerged from within the Anglo-American model of strong faculty affiliation of higher education, and have advanced from a narrow *in loco parentis* model, which primarily concerned itself with student discipline, conduct, student social and moral development, to a theoretical discipline which informs a normative meta-framework supported by rigorous research and prolific publications (Pascarella & Terenzini 2005). In a review on the trends of student affairs in the USA, Fang and Wu (2006: 6) commented that

> [t]he relationship between student affairs and academic affairs in the US higher education institutions has undergone the spiral evolution from original natural unification to conscious differentiation and independence, and later moving towards collaborative and integrating educational partnership. Such a development course reflects not only the inner logical demands for continuous professional and academic growth of student affairs in American universities, but also the profound changes in its basic aim, conception, concrete mission and role orientation.

Student affairs practitioners in the USA today are professionals, typically with masters and doctoral level qualifications in educational leadership, and part of an education faculty of a university (Keeling 2004; Nuss 2003; Schuh 2003). The American student affairs practitioner takes part in the core business of higher education by 'working effectively with faculty to create a coherent curriculum' (Schuh 2003: 73).

In the USA, as the higher education focus shifted from educating the elite to 'building a nation', student affairs divisions were positioned as key role-players in contributing to the core mission, by producing rigorous research and demonstrating their impact (Nuss 2003: 67). While positivistic demonstrations of outcome and impact present ideological challenges, perhaps emulating the USA is a trajectory South African student affairs might follow.

Australian and UK student affairs divisions are similar to the USA model of viewing student affairs as a profession which significantly contributes to institutional goals through holistic student development and has 'much to contribute to maintaining and improving student retention' (Burke 1997; Trainor 2002: 4). Trainor (2002) notes the shift in the UK from perceptions of student affairs as a welfare service, a 'reactive support department' which is the 'last resort for students with problems' to the perception that student affairs is the 'first port of call involved in supporting all students', which is 'fundamental to the work of the HEI as a whole' (Trainor 2002: 11). The professionalisation of student affairs has contributed much to the perception of student affairs as key contributor to the work of higher education as a whole.

Europe

Mainland Europe, reflecting the Roman-Continental higher education model, has a rather young student affairs history (Du Toit 2007). Mainland Europe only began addressing student life, student development, student services and student support as part of university life in earnest during the 1950s (Nuss 2003). During the 19th century, German universities in particular promoted an exclusively academic focus in the university, based on the highly contested notion of the 'value-free academic ethos' (Dalton 1999: 5).

Currently, European student affairs are explicit about their values and principles and include a focus on services such as counselling, disability, childcare, career development, accommodation support, sports and others (UNESCO 2004). Some student affairs are separate from the core business of the university and located in local government or municipal services, where funding and accountability lines are shared between the institution and the local or national government, or public social services[8]. This has been increasingly overshadowed by a shift towards internationalisation of higher education, promoting and enabling student mobility and exchanges, not only across the European Higher Education Area, but also with institutions abroad (Figel 2009). The Bologna Process, the UK Ministerial Initiative (PMI) and the ERASMUS agreement (European Community Scheme for the Mobility of University Students) assist in dissolving cultural boundaries and political borders and promote large-scale student mobility precipitating a focus on the role of student affairs in facilitating this mobility (Dalton 1999; Figel 2009).

The challenges for student affairs in the developed world centre around student affairs' relationship with the community within which it defines itself and to which it relates. There appear trends around utilising student affairs as a tool towards enhancing the overall student experience of students, particularly exchange and 'mobile' students, often with a focus on enhancing the competitive edge of universities. This might overshadow student affairs' contract with society, with community and with the larger social good. According to Kezar (2004), student affairs may not lose this focus on developing students which have a keen awareness of the systemic social 'embeddedness' and their relationship with local communities, while at the same time engaging with global issues. This tension remains a challenge for student affairs in the Bologna Zone but also extends beyond it.

Student affairs in developing regions

Countries with developing democracies and developing economies share many issues, particularly around higher education. Student affairs divisions within developing countries and economies are not as professionalised and explicitly articulated as student affairs in the developed world.

Brazil, India and China

In a similar way to South Africa, higher education in Brazil was designed to support the economic and political elite and was tightly controlled by a military regime (Sidhu 2006). Today, Brazil is facing similar challenges to South Africa: the need to produce 'equity, quality and efficiency' (Sidhu 2006: 283). Like South Africa, Brazil's dilemma is to produce research which attracts international interest while finding solutions to local problems (Buroway 2010; Carnoy 2002; Cloete & Muller 1998; Sidhu 2006). Brazil, like India, is focused on promoting international student mobility along North–South and South–South lines, and student affairs in these contexts are frequently geared towards supporting these goals.

India's educational system, owing to its colonial roots, is much like South Africa's. The Anglo-Saxon system of higher education informed the basic structure of the institutions and student affairs within it (Chitnis 2000; Du Toit 2007). India, like most of the rest of the developing world, is engaged in improving access and equity across higher education to become an 'economic powerhouse' (Punwani, cited in Gupta 2006: 2). India is struggling with a deeply entrenched caste system and, like South Africa, is trying to redress the injurious effects of its colonial and political history. Of great interest is India's attempt to improve access of the different 'castes' to higher education (Gupta 2006).

While there are pockets of excellence, such as the All India Institute for Medical Science, largely supported by specific federal funding, corporate interest and 'educational entrepreneurs of a new breed', it seems that, overall, the Indian higher education sector is burdened by inequities, challenges around implementation, poor accountability, under-funding, dated pedagogical practices, student unrest, migration of students to first-world universities, and other factors deeply rooted in the historical, cultural and social norms (George & Raman 2009: 3).

Despite much reference to the interpersonal and social difficulties, such as racism and discrimination, integration and social cohesion, first-generation student epistemological access challenges to higher education, and mainstream student tolerance to students on 'reserved seats', student affairs seems to not feature on the Indian higher education landscape (George & Raman 2009; Thornton, Bricheno, Iyer, Reid, Wankhede & Green 2010). It seems that offices which facilitate 'training and placement' for career purposes are largely private and outside the institutional structures. Some student affairs-type services appear on websites and brochures, but remain isolated examples restricted to flagship institutions. Student governance seems to have a presence at some university websites (e.g., the University of Hyderabad and Rajiv Gandhi University), as do international mobility, cultural festivities and sports activities, such as cricket and basketball[9].

During the 1970s, China adopted a new stance towards education, with a move away from the Maoist centralist model to decentralisation, which gave local authority the autonomy and flexibility to create more opportunities for access and to respond to societal needs, while improving relations with Western higher education institutions (Liu, Rhoads & Wang 2007). By the 1980s, formal agreements on educational exchange and collaboration with the West were quite common for higher education institutions in China (Liu *et al.* 2007; Loeftstedt & Shangwu 2002).

The development of student affairs in higher education in China 'does not seem to represent the result of systemic or strategic planning at the highest level' (Wang 2004: 9). Initially, a division named Student Residences and Career Services was introduced, which later morphed into student affairs. China's academic disciplines seem to engender a sense of belonging (Wang 2004), reminiscent of the original student affairs model of *in loco parentis*, where academic staff were entrusted with moral and professional caretaking of their protégés.

While some high-ranking flagship universities, such as Peking University and Beijing Normal University, offer a range of student services, student societies, student volunteering and counselling and health care[10], little literature is available on Chinese student affairs models and theories (UNESDOC 2002; Wang 2004). It appears that 'little attention is being paid to either the theoretical or practical aspects of facilitating student development through student affairs programs and services' (Wang 2004: 11).

The African continent

African universities are as young as Africa's independence from colonial powers, bar the few established by the ex-patriot communities and colonialists. As Mamdani states, Africa 'became independent with no more than a handful of university graduates in the population' (Mamdani, cited in Du Toit 2007: 56). To promote African independence and African nation-building, the 'university functioned as an integral part of the post-independence African nationalist movement' (Mamdani, cited in Du Toit 2007: 56).

Higher education institutions across Africa grapple with issues similar to South African universities. Throughout Africa, as in South Africa, the university is considered a key contributor to national development and is reflected in student enrolment which has increased five-fold in the late 20th century across the African continent (Za'rour 1998).

In general, African student affairs divisions follow the USA model of a student affairs domain with a focus on student development, student support and student services for holistic student development aligned with the institutional goals, such as Strathmore University in Kenya and the University of Zambia[11]. African student affairs domains are staffed by a dean of students with a complement of staff focusing on 'planning, coordinating and implementing a variety of programmes and services which are designed to assist and support students in achieving academic and personal success'[12]. Some universities embrace models of integrated student development and speak of developing 'a conducive learning and living environment'[13]. Younger universities, such as the University of The Gambia, seem to have international offices addressing issues of student mobility[14]. Overall, the influence of the USA on African student affairs as comprehensive and integrated, and aimed at holistic student development, with a pronounced focus on internationalisation, is evident across the African continent.

In addition to the focus, among others, on promoting internationalisation, student affairs practitioners in Africa also address urgent and compelling social concerns resulting from injurious social-political practices within and beyond higher education. The African Student Affairs Conference (ASAC 2009, 2010, 2011) hosted university deans and student affairs professionals of African universities, and the papers which were presented revealed that the student affairs domains focus on issues around campus conflicts, race and gender violence, and basic problems of living, such as food and housing[15]. However, the conference papers do not shed much light on the scope, role and function of African student affairs, on frameworks and theories, and conceptual issues around student affairs philosophy (ASAC 2009, 2010, 2011).

Literature and research concerning student affairs issues in Africa appear sparse and appear only rarely in international journals. The only Africa-wide journal in which student affairs is also covered is the *Journal of Higher Education in Africa*, published irregularly by CODESRIA (Council for the Development of Social Science Research in Africa, located in Senegal). Some African universities (e.g. Makerere University, Kenya) publish frequent education faculty-based in-house journals. More recently, online Nigerian journals have appeared, such as the *International Journal of Educational Research*, but without a clear continental focus. Recently the first edition of the *Journal of Student Affairs in Africa* has been published, which aims to fill this gap.

The review of student affairs in the developing world reveals that there is little coherent collective framework for student affairs either at national level or across the developing world. The need for a theoretical framework informing student affairs structural integration and concrete engagements seems pronounced.

Lessons learnt from developed and developing regions

In summary, the USA sets the benchmark for student affairs internationally, and has developed a coherent epistemological community. Based on rigorous research, it conceptualises student affairs as 'working effectively with faculty in creating a coherent curriculum in which specified learning outcomes are achieved through collaboration' (Schuh 2003: 73). It is characterised by the integration of student affairs into the organisational structure and academic experience at faculty level (Kuh *et al.* 2010; Kuh 1995; Pascarella & Terenzini 2005). European models of student affairs locate student affairs within Bernstein's 'official recontextualising field' of higher education, where it contributes to administrative service delivery, which is beyond the boundaries of the academic domain (Bernstein 2000).

The review of the international student affairs reveals a medley of structures and frameworks, and this diversity reflects the myriad of contexts into which student affairs is embedded. The articulation of student affairs to its immediate context is essential and this is expressed succinctly by Manning, Kinzie and Schuh's book on student affairs organisational structures and innovative models entitled *One Size Does Not Fit All* (2006). The importance of the role of student affairs in preserving the relationship with its context remains a key challenge and objective for student affairs within the developed and the developing world.

It appears essential that student affairs organises itself into a coherent discipline and focuses on local theory development which can inform an integrated, comprehensive, locally-relevant conceptual framework so that it can articulate effectively with the academic domain in creating a 'coherent curriculum'.

Influences of internationalisation on student affairs

Traditional boundaries of student affairs are expanding and internationalisation is described as the 'new frontier for student affairs' (Dalton 1999: 3). Quiang (2003) describes various aspects of internationalisation which affect student affairs: a) internationalisation as an aim in itself, with special focus on multiculturalism as a value in student development; b) internationalisation as a vehicle to achieve broader goals, such as improved employability; c) reshaping student affairs to accommodate international students; and d) internationalisation as a culture and ethos beyond student affairs to enable engagement in the global arena and to compete on the global market. These aspects of internationalisation affect student affairs differently.

In Europe, the Bologna Process has had a huge impact with its emphasis on mobility, employability and competitiveness. The 'social dimension' is increasingly becoming a 'necessary condition for the attractiveness and competitiveness of the EHEA' (Eurostat 2009). This directly impacts on student affairs as it is considered to contribute towards an institution's attractiveness and competitive advantage rather than, perhaps, focusing on its 'contract with society'.

Internationalisation is viewed as an enriching experience for students (Cloete 2009), and countries recognise the economic value of higher education internationalisation as a revenue-producing industry (Dalton 1999; Merrick 2007). Dalton (1999) pointed out that international discourse on student mobility is expressed not only in actual international student numbers but also in the revenue these students generate (Dalton 1999). Perhaps a risk in defining international students in economic terms is the resulting image of the international student as a 'cash cow', being offered special services and privileges, thus potentially compromising student affairs' ethical principles. It appears that ethics, values, and social implications of internationalisation are neglected and consumer-related discourses overwhelm the domain (Kelly 2009).

The UK Council on International Student Affairs (UKCISA) has identified a list of key deliverables for student affairs in order to enhance the international student experience (Merrick 2007; UKCISA 1999). This is an illustrative example of the shift in thinking about student affairs: student affairs is involved in making the higher education experience more attractive to improve mobility, and in this way contributes to its economic viability. Student affairs is called upon to deliver on factors which increase student satisfaction, as a marketing strategy (Garci'a-Aracil 2009; Merrik 2007; UKCISA 1999). For instance, the I-Graduate Student Barometer is used as a tool to measure student satisfaction, and the results are used to inform student affairs within some institutions with the purpose of attracting more students to the university (Merrick 2007).

Lessons learnt from internationalisation

Internationalisation and the dissolution of educational borders will continue to increase and, for instance, student affairs in the Bologna Zone has harnessed the opportunities emerging from the increased student mobility. International student affairs will need to go beyond the focus on mobility and contribute to the emerging discourse on globalisation, including ubiquitously used but loosely defined terms such as 'global citizenship' and in that way overcome the 'parochial' dualism of global and local (Cloete & Muller 1998).

Internationalisation is also about a change in culture and ethos of student affairs (Quaing 2003). This might take the form of engaging in formal relations with international associations of student affairs. North–South and South–South collaborations might assist in engaging indigenous knowledge which might be more or differently relevant to the South African context, especially given the ubiquitous readiness to embrace well-developed American theories and models. Moreover, in terms of alignment and framework, the associations in the European Higher Education Area (EHEA), such as the European Council for Student Affairs, offer insight into student affairs structural alignments and constellations involving the state. This refers to the different trajectories of student affairs constellations in the Anglo-Saxon and Continental-Roman education models and the post-colonial discourse on the instrumentalist university and its role in the African nationalist movement. This might be an opportunity to move the student affairs lens beyond the nation-state towards a globalised sense of ethics and morals (Nussbaum 1997). The engagements with international associations around a shared discourse on ethics and morals might facilitate South African student affairs' explicit articulation of its position in this regard.

The quest for a normative framework

The review of international student affairs suggests that student affairs in developing regions has not developed a locally relevant conceptual framework for student affairs. South African as much as other developing and some developed countries, might benefit from developing a normative framework which can maintain central vision and reduce the random mushrooming of often privatised student affairs functions. Detached and fragmented student affairs, as is found in developing and some developed international regions, might risk derailment of vision and neglect theory and best-practice principles or might pose high risk to the institution and side-step accountability. This needs to hold the tension with potentially rigid centralist control, encumbered by bloated bureaucracies which prevent flexible responsiveness to faculty needs.

This tension between the generic and central, on the one hand, and the specific and narrow, on the other, needs to be explicitly negotiated in order to preserve the underlying values and principles of student affairs. A principle- and value-based framework located within a theoretical paradigm[16] can provide guidance for Student affairs domains which look towards professionalisation.

A key lesson which a review of the international research on student affairs provides is the integration of student affairs into the institutional life. Based on research primarily emerging on the international, mainly USA, landscape, but increasingly also from South Africa, is the widely accepted assertion that student affairs' contribution to higher education is predicated on its integration into the core business of the institution (King & Baxter-Magolda 1996; Kuh et al. 2010; Pascarella & Terenzini 2005; Perry 1970; Davidowitz & Schreiber 2008; SAACDHE 2007; Schuh 2003).

Theory which underpins student affairs asserts that 'cognitive and affective dimensions of development are related parts of one process' (Astin 1977; Baxter-Magolda 1992; Feldman Smart & Ethington 2004; King & Baxter-Magolda 1996: 163; Kuh & Hu 2001; Kuh et al. 2010; Nuss 2003; Pascarella & Terenzini 2005; Tinto 1997). The construction and use of knowledge is related to the student's sense of self and self-authorship in the higher education institution. This is also expressed by King and Baxter-Magolda (1996: 165) who assert that 'the known is inextricably connected to the knower'. Epistemological access is grounded in the active construction of knowledge (Bernstein 2000), that is, the active interpretation of experience.

These theoretical principles of student affairs suggest a re-definition of learning as a broad process across cognitive, affective, and social domains. Learning is synergistic, not segmented (Nuss 2003; Weiderman 1989). Hence student affairs' theoretical and structural articulation is vital.

Professionalising an emerging discipline

The challenges for student affairs nationally and internationally, especially in developing countries, are not only about how to develop well-defined and relevant interventions with explicit outcomes, aligned with institutional and national educational imperatives, but also about how to establish itself as a discipline and a profession[17] and articulate a coherent meta-framework.

The USA student affairs domain has generated a significant and rigorous body of research, has developed seminal theories, established a recognised discipline, managed to professionalise itself and form broad and inclusive associations which reflect the texture and depth of student affairs in the USA (Dean 2006; Keeling 2004; Nuss 2003; Pascarella & Terenzini 2005; Schuh 2003; Strayhorn 2006). This might be a trajectory South African student affairs might follow.

The move towards a professionalised discipline for countries which need to harness divergent voices into a coherent epistemological community, might require the support of organised associations. These might take on the form of 'issue networks', which share knowledge about particular issues or problems, or 'epistemic communities', which form a network of experts who can exert influence on the basis of knowledge and research, or 'advocacy coalitions', which exert pressure over a period of time through co-ordinated activity (Bailey[18] 2010: 14). Along with student affairs associations, it is especially non-governmental organisations such as the Centre for Higher Education Transformation which may be able to play a key role in this regard.

For student affairs in developing countries, it appears imperative to engage in local theory development and critically engage with established theoretical frameworks. Student affairs in South Africa, as in other developing countries, requires a normative meta-framework that accommodates multiple indigenous realities which need to flourish in a global context. The capabilities approach[19] (Sen 1995, 2001) and the principles of the ethics of care (Gilligan 1981, 1982; Nussbaum 1995, 1997, 2000) seem particularly useful in enabling contextual, constructivist and narrative thinking in a pluralist context such as South African higher education[20].

Influences of globalisation on student affairs

Buroway (2010: 1) referred to South African universities burdened by apartheid inequities and those that need to compete in a global reality as 'under-resourced at one end and subject to global competition on the other' and 'caught between the disabling legacies of the past and the structural pressures of the present'

(Buroway 2010: 1). Perhaps Buroway's distinction is artificial and the burden of an exploitative and injurious past and the need to compete globally reflects a reality into which many national and international universities are embedded.

Castells (2001) describes globalisation[21] as the paramount social phenomenon of recent times. This echoes Chomsky (1999), who states that 'neoliberalism[22] is the defining political economic paradigm of our time' (Chomsky, 1999: 7). Globalisation, and its economic neo-liberal influences, has a defining impact on higher education and hence also on student affairs (Castells 2001; Kezar 2004; Lange 2010). The 'discourse of globalisation positions higher education institutions as key agents in the development of graduates with the expertise and high-level skills for a high growth path of economic development and global competitiveness' (CHE 2010: 49). The eco-political changes have a particular impact on funding and resource distribution, directly affecting student affairs.

Luescher-Mamashela (2008) described the 'market-oriented university', which is structured as a 'commercial educational service provider that competes in the local (and global) higher education market' (Luescher-Mamashela 2008: 63). Students are targeted as 'clients', passive, demanding and expecting future returns. The consumed commodity leads to gainful employment and student affairs-type student development is perceived as 'distractions' unless incentivised or branded as improving chances of employment (Luescher-Mamashela 2008: 63). In these kinds of contexts student affairs is conceptualised to buttress the promise of individualised notions of graduate success (Burke 1997).

This insidious global change needs to alert student affairs to its role in contributing not only to student and institutional success but also to the common social good (Harper 1996; Kezar 2004). This 'contract with society' is also described by Kezar (2004), who emphasised that student affairs has a tradition of serving the public good and needs to remain focused on this contract with society[23].

Lessons learnt from globalisation

The commercialisation of higher education, beginning in the 1980s, has led to 'expanding industry-university collaborations' (Buroway 2010: 3), with the consequence of reduced state funding. The reduction of state funding, globally, has led to changes in the higher education and in student affairs (Buroway 2010; Hirt 2006).

Reduced state funding has led to inflated tuition fees, which affects students directly and is incompatible with the emerging democracies' claims of massification and broadening access (Schuh 2003). The higher education sector, including student affairs, is compelled to seek funding from private sources.

Commercialisation and market-driven curricula and outcomes of programmes pose some challenges to student affairs. Kezar (2004: 439) noted 'that neoliberal philosophy was one of the main forces driving the move away from the traditional charter between higher education and society, a tradition built on a communitarian philosophy of the public good'. She maintained that this tension might compromise some student affairs areas in that Student affairs survival is contingent on market-driven values (Kezar 2004). Narrow co-curricula and out-of-classroom experiences, aligned with market forces, neglect the contract with society around producing students who take part in public life and realise their social 'embeddedness', rather than just acquiring a career as a vehicle for self-promotion (Buroway 2010; ESU 2008; ISAP 2009; Kezar 2004; Sidhu 2006; Urbanski 2009).

International shifts in student affairs are evident in its increased focus on revenue-producing partnerships, for instance with bursary providers, sponsors, or 'wealthy' academic departments, its increase in programmes for international students as a client market, promoting certain brands on campus and using sports as marketing, its quasi-outsourced services, and its focus on generating lavish events to improve funders' social responsibility indicators, and so on (Dalton 1999).

While student affairs was previously accountable to the institution's goals, national goals, and society's goals, it seems that student affairs has become increasingly aligned with sponsors' goals rather than with student affairs' goals per se. Furthermore, this kind of shift makes students 'consumers' and 'clients' rather than 'participants' in the higher education process (Buroway 2010; ESU 2008; Gupta 2006; ISAP 2009; Sidhu 2006; Urbanski 2009).

The relationship with corporate partners needs to be explicitly managed in order to prevent essentialising and commercialising student affairs functions within the institutions. The trend in the USA towards the privatisation of some student affairs functions (Schuh 2003) has left these Student affairs functions voiceless in participating equitably and reciprocally within the institution. This is a trend which challenges student affairs globally and South Africa can learn key lessons from the experiences of its peers in the international terrain.

Conclusion

The challenges discussed in this paper highlight the importance of a dynamic and reciprocal relationship of student affairs with its context. The fluid context of the international higher education landscape demands that student affairs engage with global realities in a reciprocal way, simultaneously being shaped while also shaping the international terrain.

The key challenges for student affairs, especially in the developing world, are to urgently address the results of injurious social and political practices within and beyond higher education affecting students' cognitive and social-emotional functioning. Furthermore, key challenges include addressing issues of organisational and structural positioning, of framework and local theory development, engaging proactively and coherently with globalisation and internationalisation, and to professionalising and developing an epistemological community.

The professionalisation of the theoretical discipline and normative practice of student affairs is the key difference between the 'developed' and 'developing' world in terms of student affairs' integration and function within higher education. South African student affairs, perhaps guided by its various associations and assisted by non-governmental organisations such as the Centre for Higher Education Transformation, or parastatals such as the Council on Higher Education, is at an opportune moment to articulate a normative meta-framework for student affairs.

One of the stages in the maturation process of student affairs in the USA is 'differentiation and independence' (Fang & Wu 2006: 6). South African student affairs seem to find itself at a similar stage and might follow the American trajectory of maturing into a coherent theoretical discipline which articulates its structural position and utilitarian function within higher education.

The discussion on internationalisation and globalisation reveals that South African student affairs is at an fortuitous moment in which to engage with a globalised sense of ethics and morals which may inform its conceptualisation within higher education (Nussbaum 1997).

Since the surge of research and literature from within and about the student affairs in higher education (Botha, Brand, Cilliers, Davidow, de Jager & Smith 2005; Hamrick, Evans & Schuh 2002; Pascarella & Terenzini 2005) student affairs have increasingly become 'self-conscious, confident and widely influential' (Nuss 2003: 87). Student affairs in South Africa is beginning to carve an identity for itself, informed by theory and local research, and as a significant contributor to the core business of higher education.

Notes

1. The reference to the 'developed' and 'developing' world is a false dualism but is used here to cluster the themes.
2. The European Higher Education Area's Bologna Process literature has been prolific in debating pluralist values in a local context, acknowledging global values while remaining indigenous, and identifying the tensions emerging from this (www.ehea.info, accessed 10 August 2012). Cloete (1998) also raised these issues in his exploration of post-colonial discourses which might assist in

moving beyond parochial dualist notions towards pluralism anchored in globalised consciousness.
3. The reference to the 'developed' and 'developing' world is a false dualism but is used here to cluster the themes.
4. The changes for student affairs are not only systemic, but also include issues such as student profile changes, and embracing the e-medium for service delivery and engagement. Kretovics (2003) presents an interesting review in *The role of student affairs in distance education: Cyber-services or virtual communities*, which highlights that the changed context also includes migrating some Student Affairs roles and functions to the virtual and online media, given that talk-and-chalk didactics have been replaced by innovative pedagogies which include the idea that learning takes place in virtual spaces. New communications technologies have a 'profound influence on the way students, professors, administrator and staff live, study, work and do their business on and off campus' (Grant, 1999: 59).
5. http://www.iasasonline.org/ (accessed 10 August 2012)
6. http://www.iasasonline.org/ (accessed 8 August 2012)
7. The Continental-Roman model has nonetheless constitutionally protected academic freedom. But, as Du Toit pointed out, this is only of any value in so far as the state observes the constitution, which was not the case in, for instance, Nazi Germany (Du Toit 2007).
8. www.direct.gov.de (accessed 8 August 2012), www.studentenwerk.de (accessed 10 August 2012)
9. www.rgu.ac.in (accessed 10 August 2012); www.uohyd.ernet.in (accessed 10 August 2012); www.du.ac.in (accessed 10 August 2012)
10. http://english.pku.edu.cn/ (accessed 10 August 2012) and www.bnu.edu.cn (accessed 10 August 2012)
11. www.strathmore.edu (accessed 10 August 2012); www.unza.zm (accessed 10 August 2012)
12. www.strathmore.edu/dos (accessed 10 August 2012)
13. www.unza.zm (accessed 10 August 2012)
14. www.unigambia.gm (accessed 8 August 2012)
15. The student affairs discourse apparent at the ASAC revealed a ubiquitous use of 'training' and 'skills' which apparently is aimed to affect behaviour and attitudinal changes in students. The terms 'training' and 'skills' are premised on assumptions that access to higher education culture can be taught in discrete units, which is not supported by international research and reflects a simplistic and reductionist understanding of student affairs scope, role, function and practice.
16. Various international resources are useful to assist in the development of a South African normative framework. The *Council for the Advancement of Standards in Higher Education* (Dean, 2006) is a particularly useful resource in this regard.
17. A 'profession' has to do with the scope of practice and behaviours associated with a profession, while 'professionalism' refers to the implicit or explicit code of conduct and norms associated with a profession.
18. Bailey (2010) discussed the policy-research nexus and explored the utilisation of research and its impact on policy and in particular the role 'networks' (such as associations) in terms of the interplay between research and policy.
19. The human capabilities approach was originally developed by Amartya Sen (1984, 1995, 2001) and has since been a leading paradigm for policy development around human development issues and was the basis for the United Nations Human Development Index.
20. South African higher education is governed by a policy context which constructs 'Student Development and Support' (the equivalent to student affairs) in a particular way, and any meta-framework needs to comply with national policy. The *National Commission on Higher Education: An overview of a new policy framework for higher education transformation* (DoE, 1996: 12) is particularly informative in this regard.
21. *Globalisation* means the global mobility and transnational circulation of information, education,

culture and economics, through the increase in exchange and the opening of borders by the reduction of barriers and the increase of open access to information via the internet and other virtual platforms.

22. The term *neoliberalism* was coined to describe the period after socio-economic liberalism, which dominated the first world with its emphasis on civil liberty and economic freedom, while protecting individual rights. The removal of the protective regulations sheltering economic monopolies is considered the onset of the neoliberal economic order.

23. Du Toit (2007) discusses the issues arising from considering, what he called, higher education's 'social contract'. He argued that the social contract safeguards academic freedom and self-determination, a key element for student affairs within the institutions.

An overview of critical issues in the student affairs profession: A South African perspective

Llewellyn MacMaster
University of Stellenbosch

Summary

Drawing on the insights of Sandeen and Barr (2006) as well as the National Development Plan, the Strategic Plan of the Department of Higher Education and Training and other relevant documents, this paper reflects on some of the critical issues facing student affairs in general, and practitioners within the South African context in particular. Acknowledging the complexity of the South African context, the article reflects on broader national as well as more specific institutional issues that present themselves as challenges and opportunities for student affairs. Such challenges include questions pertaining to the profession itself as well as to critical issues and challenges in the field of work as experienced specifically by student affairs practitioners in South Africa. Ultimately student affairs professionals are cautioned to guard against self-marginalisation within the higher education sector. Student affairs units are urged to claim their rightful and crucial role in the total learning experience of students.

Introduction

The current context of higher education presents student affairs with many challenges. 'The ever-changing role of student affairs has now become more complex due to diversity of age, ethnic, academic and financial backgrounds of students' (Lumadi & Mampuru 2010: 716). These challenges are not limited to our South African context. The 1998 World Declaration on Higher Education (WDHE) lists the following challenges:

> financing, equality of access, widening participation, the improvement of support and developmental services, effective use of technology (including distance learning), use of new and more flexible learning formats, ensuring student attainment of new skills and increased employability, as well as the need for international co-operation. (UNESCO 2002: 8)

Student affairs professionals and practitioners play a very important role in institutions of higher learning. They are strategically placed to engage with students in a meaningful way to bring together 'in-class' and 'out-of-class' experiences and to enhance the total learning experience of students, fulfilling the aim of higher education in general, namely to develop well-rounded graduates. Student affairs practitioners are also best placed within institutions to ensure that the holistic and integrated development and care of students are taken seriously and applied. To be able to play this critical role, student affairs professionals have to take themselves and their work seriously, continuously re-evaluating what they are doing, speak with authority and guard against self-marginalisation. They have the opportunity to be partners in the academic project to educate students in the South Africa of the 21st century, 'who will have to contend with increasingly perilous social circumstances', but also 'extraordinary possibilities for transforming our world into one that is socially just, compassionate and environmentally responsible' (Waghid 2011: 5). However, appreciation and acknowledgment of their position and role as partners are crucial in order for institutions and the higher education sector to deliver on their mandate. This is a key element in the paper and it will surface at various points in the discussion.

The critical issues discussed here do not represent an absolute or complete list, but they stem from my personal reflection as a student affairs professional at Stellenbosch University and as secretary general of the South African Association for Senior Student affairs Professionals (SAASSAP) for the last four years.

This paper discusses a proposal for the foundation of the student affairs profession and looks at the vital role the transformation agenda plays within the higher education sector and within the broader socio-political context of South Africa. It then focuses on the financial needs and the challenges faced by many students who have put their hopes in attaining a degree as a means to a better life. The discussion then moves to the importance of cultivating and developing ethical leadership as a way to build credibility for the profession. The discussion is concluded by pointing the way forward for student affairs professionals and practitioners, as well as listing a number of challenges.

The foundation of the student affairs profession

Sandeen and Barr (2006: 1) correctly identify the question about the foundation of student affairs as the first critical issue for consideration by student affairs professionals. In their view,

> [t]he foundation of any profession is formed from a shared philosophy about what needs to be done, a shared understanding of the theoretical constructs that inform the practice of the profession, the application of the accumulated knowledge of the members to the tasks that need to be accomplished, and the ability of the practitioners of the profession to effectively link their theoretical knowledge, practical wisdom, and skills to larger organizations and society.

The strong foundations of any profession do not just occur by accident or seem to appear overnight. 'They are the result of hard work, careful planning, examination of strengths and weaknesses, and the provision of needed reinforcement at critical times' (Sandeen & Barr 2006: 2).

The authors trace the development of a shared foundation for the student affairs profession in the USA with reference to its philosophical and theoretical foundations, organisational theories and implications for graduate preparation programmes. Given the diverse nature of student affairs and the fact that it is continuing to grow and evolve, multiple perspectives and theories should be encouraged. Two 'enduring and distinctive concepts' continue to form the foundation of the profession, namely 'the consistent and persistent commitment to the development of the whole person' and the fact that student affairs 'support[s] the academic mission of the college' (Sandeen & Barr 2006: 3).

Unlike the well-documented history of student affairs in the United States of America, which marks the profession's development into becoming an integral part of higher education, South Africa lacks a significant library of evidence that traces the development of the profession. The volume edited by Martin Mandew, *A Guide to Student Services in South Africa* (2003) provides an important and crucial contribution in this regard. SAASSAP, representing student affairs professionals in most of the 23 public universities in South Africa, for example, has only been in existence for a decade and a half. There is also currently an attempt to establish an umbrella body for the different national associations representing various sectors in student affairs and student development[1]. One of the main motivations for having such an umbrella body is to have a stronger voice and more coordination of associations, hopefully resulting in greater professionalisation and utilisation of resources, and ultimately a more efficient service delivery to students in all tertiary institutions. In addition, student affairs professionals are a very diverse group of people. Their role as professionals in their own right is also not always acknowledged within their respective institutions and the higher education sector in general. One common feeling among professionals and practitioners in student affairs is one of being the fire brigade that is called upon to extinguish or at least dampen student protest, with too little appreciation of the overall critical work being done consistently year in and year out.

There is a general sense that each institution treats student affairs according to local needs and challenges, with the result that no clear 'South African' model has emerged. This is evident in the titles of those who head divisions, departments or centres for student affairs. These range from executive director, dean of students to director, who may report directly to senior directors, or to the registrar or to a deputy vice-chancellor. Some are part of the institution's top management, either as members or in an advisory capacity, while others report to a member of the management team.

Not all divisions (departments, centres) for student affairs are constituted in the same way, making benchmarking a difficult exercise. Student affairs professionals should lead the discussion regarding the placement of student affairs in the organisational structure 'with vigour and forthrightness' (Sandeen & Barr 2006: 30). They cannot leave it up to 'those with little or no knowledge of, or commitment to student affairs' to make decisions about the organisational status of student affairs. Student affairs practitioners have to guard against self-marginalisation. One sure way to ensure that student affairs practitioners are part of the conversations, deliberations and decision-making processes in their institutions is to adhere to one of the two 'enduring and distinctive concepts' referred to earlier, namely to 'support the academic mission of the college' (Sandeen & Barr 2006: 3). We are important stakeholders and partners driving one of the strategic objectives of institutions of higher learning: student success.

To a large extent, the work of student affairs practitioners is still seen as providing services that complement and facilitate the learning process (Hamrick, Evans & Shuh 2002: 113). However, this view should not be accepted as the last word on student affairs. Student learning outside the classroom is busy evolving 'from a peripheral experience to a central part of the educational experience'

(Hamrick, Evans and Shuh 2002: 113). The seminal work of Pascarella and Terenzini, *How College Affects Students* (1991), has played a major role in broadening our thinking about a total learning experience and the importance of systematically and purposefully integrating the students' academic and social lives in order to enhance their learning. This broadened understanding of learning is articulated by Keeling (2004: 5) as follows: 'Learning is a complex, holistic, multi-centric activity that occurs throughout and across the college experience.' In this sense we speak about 'co-curricular', rather than 'extra-curricular' activities and learning opportunities, consciously shifting the focus of our role as student affairs practitioners from the margins to the centre. It implies combining activity (merely running around doing things and rendering services, which in any event remain an integral part of our work) with critical reflection, study and research. This will empower student affairs professionals and practitioners to provide important input into the institution's strategic plans regarding curriculum development, community engagement, budget, facilities management, etc.

The various models for the organisation of student affairs will indeed continue to be debated. I agree with the assessment of Sandeen and Barr (2006: 48) that the most important issue for student affairs 'is not where it is placed on the organizational chart, but how effective its leadership is on campus.'

Finding some common or shared foundation for student affairs in South Africa will be a critical step in helping to establish the profession. Mandew (2003: 21) rightfully postulates that right now there is 'no overtly articulated philosophical framework or explicit theory that informs practice in the field of student services' in South Africa. This is a huge challenge. Professionals in student affairs come from a diverse academic background (psychology, theology, education, etc.) and need to utilise their scientific knowledge to develop the necessary theoretical foundations for student affairs within the South African context.

Unlike the USA the field of student affairs in South Africa has not evolved to the level of being a formal academic discipline for qualification purposes. There have been some developments in this regard, with the University of the Western Cape (UWC) collaborating with the University of California Fullerton to design a PhD course, with the first student registering in 2011. The Southern African Chapter of the Association of College and University Housing Officers – International (ACUHO-I) has also recently started, with professional training courses for its members. It is encouraging that a number of colleagues in the field are busy with or completing doctoral studies that focus on student affairs. A greater emphasis is also placed on research papers, in addition to presentations on best practices at conferences. It is hoped that this will be beneficial and enriching, not only to the student affairs sector, but to higher education as well.

Mandew (2003: 21) proposes a 'critical paradigm' for student affairs which points in the direction of a foundational principle for the profession in South Africa. He asserts that student services practice in South Africa is largely influenced by 'a de facto hybridisation of the inherited *in loco parentis* and intellectualist approaches', lacking a common philosophical framework with an increasing tendency towards managerialism, rather than being education-orientated and development-focused. The challenge for student services practitioners, according to Mandew, 'is to develop and maintain a healthy tension between the need for sound technical management driven by financial efficiencies and bottom-line priorities on one hand, and a progressive and creative student-centred and development-oriented focus driven by educational imperatives on the other' (2003: 22).

The following elements are therefore of critical importance in the discussion about the foundation of the student affairs profession:

- Student affairs plays a fundamental role in the core function (academic mission) of higher education institutions, namely teaching and learning, research, and community engagement.
- Student affairs is best positioned to ensure that institutions fulfil their objective with regard to graduate attributes, 'delivering' the graduates that will make the best possible contribution to society. A key factor here is the intentional bringing together of the curricular (or in-class) learning and the co-curricular (out-of-class) learning to create a total learning experience for students. Student affairs practitioners should be experts in reading and interpreting matters and developments pertaining to the life and learning of students.
- Professional development of student affairs practitioners is a given. Taking into account that disciplines such as student counselling and health services have already established professional bodies, much more will have to be done in this regard.
- Developing a philosophical framework for student affairs in South Africa that undergirds the work of professionals and guide practitioners in the field is critical. This framework will draw from the global research and experience in the field, but will remain contextual.

The Principles of Good Practice for Student Affairs, drawn up jointly by two North American associations – ACPA (American College Personnel Association) and NASPA (National Association of Student Personnel Administrators) in 1997 – emphasise the importance of *context* and the appreciation of the total life experience of students for practitioners:

Our history also reminds us that good student affairs practice must be considered within the context of issues that influence higher education and its missions. Societal concerns and needs, economic conditions, and external political agendas shape the parameters for student affairs work. These conditions emphasize the need for our practices to be informed by research and writing not only about teaching and learning but also concerning the most pressing issues confronting our students and their families. (ACPA 1997: 1)

The specific socio-political and economic context of South Africa provides the background for the discussion of a number of critical issues facing student affairs.

The transformation agenda

The dawn of a democratic dispensation in South Africa in 1994 presented the country with several daunting challenges, especially with regard to the tremendous levels of inequality that are still so pervasive in society. The process of transformation is hamstrung by factors like fiscal constraints, subjected to market volatilities, encumbered by political exigencies and 'dampened by social sensitivities' (Mandew 2003: 19). It is therefore not surprising that the 'transformation agenda' is a critical part of every plan and process within institutions, organisations and government departments. The Education White Paper 3 1997 entitled 'A Programme for the Transformation of Higher Education' makes it clear that higher education 'must contribute to and support the process of societal transformation, as outlined in the then Reconstruction and Development Programme', which would lead to the building of a better quality of life for all. Higher education in South Africa undoubtedly has a responsibility to advocate for and cultivate democratic action. Universities are the places where students' minds are shaped in preparation for enacting their responsibilities as citizens in a democratic society (Waghid 2010: 491). Furthermore, the correlation between excellence in education and training and high levels of economic growth resulting in significant improvements in the living standards of the masses of people is generally recognised (Council on Higher Education 2004: 14).

Firfirey and Carolissen (2010: 988) point out that the Ministerial Committee on Social Cohesion (2008) and the report on the Summit on Higher Education (2010) have documented how many of the challenges identified in the White Paper 3 of 1997 still remain in relation to race, gender and class. This corresponds with the general view about the progress we have made in South Africa as a nation. The National Development Plan (NDP) (NPC 2011: 1) lists a number of achievements since 1994, such as the adoption of the Constitution, the establishment of institutions of democracy, the building of a non-racial and non-sexist public service, the restoration of the health of the public finances. It also declares that 'democracy has not just restored the dignity of all South Africans – it has also translated into improved access to education, health services, water, housing, electrification and social security'. The NDP identifies pervasive poverty and high levels of inequality as the key challenges for the country, with millions of people remaining unemployed and many working households still living close to the poverty line. It proposes the writing of a new story for South Africa in which young people will have 'the capabilities and confidence to grasp the opportunities of a brighter future (NPC 2011: 5). In this regard, education, training and innovation are central elements in eliminating poverty and reducing inequality. 'Education empowers people to identify their identity, take control of their lives, raise healthy families, take part confidently in developing a just society, and play an effective role in the politics and governance of their communities' (NPC 2011: 261). Universities are recognised as key to the development of a nation through education and training of people with high-level skills, producing new knowledge, and providing opportunities for social mobility and simultaneously strengthening equity, social justice and democracy (NPC 2011: 262).

As we move towards two decades of democracy under a majority government, universities in South Africa are indeed still struggling to clearly define their role in society, given the realities of 'globalisation' – 'a meaningful integration of local and global dynamics' (Brooks & Normore 2010: 53). On the one hand, the socio-economic realities of the majority of people still bear testimony to 'deeply rooted and intractable historical inequalities' (DHET 2011), access to higher education is still shockingly low, too many students entering universities are critically under-prepared, and funding for higher education is decreasing. Therefore, we still have major challenges in improving access and quality of education and educational outcomes. On the other hand, the demands of a globalised world are putting pressure on South Africa to produce graduates who will be able to compete with the best in the world. The isolation that South Africa experienced during the years of apartheid has also made way for a much more open society, both in terms of knowledge and the socio-political economy – we 'see' the world in our streets and on our campuses every day.

One of the biggest and most difficult challenges for us in South Africa since 1994 has been how to deal with our past, while simultaneously dealing with the demands of the ever-changing global world. How can we be active, serious players on the global scene, while meeting the real demands of creating a better life for all citizens, especially those who had been disadvantaged under the apartheid system? A 'greater understanding of globalization' is indeed 'relevant to the preparation and practice of contemporary educational leaders' (Brooks & Normore 2010: 53). The transformation agenda should not be discarded in the name of seeking to be a world-class university, but these two facets should rather be seen as two sides of the same coin. Helping students develop holistically, overcoming socio-economic challenges that obstruct their learning, and increasing the number of more well-rounded graduates should be the singular objective of everyone involved in universities. Waghid therefore rightly posits that 'higher education in South Africa has a responsibility to advocate for and cultivate democratic action' (Waghid 2010: 491).

Waghid continues: 'A university that abdicates its responsibility to educate for critical democratic education cannot be a university for the sole reason that it is disconnected from much-needed public change' (2010: 491). Student affairs professionals are well placed to ensure the cultivation of 'deliberative diverse spaces' (Waghid 2010: 492) through courageous conversations and daring deliberations with the possibility of coming to something new. 'A university that does not teach its students to deliberate undermines the very role of democratic education – that is, such a university fails to enact its responsibility towards nurturing a democratic society' (Waghid 2010: 492). Practically all institutions have critical and engaged citizens as one of their graduate attributes, in other words, as a desired learning outcome. Universities present students with multiple opportunities 'to exercise citizenship, empower themselves as citizens, and develop their citizen potential' (Hamrick, Evans & Shuh 2002: 181). Student affairs practitioners could assist in 'educating campus regarding the value of service learning, leadership development, and other experiences shown to contribute to citizen development' (Hamrick, Evans & Shuh 2002: 207). Many students have to engage in these deliberative diverse spaces and take part in citizenship development as so-called 'wounded healers' who are themselves 'vulnerable' persons experiencing 'perpetual institutional hegemonies of exclusion and marginalisation on the basis of race and class', which does not do much to enhance students' feeling of belonging (Waghid 2010: 492).

In the next section I discuss the impact of continuing societal inequalities, as evidenced in high levels of unemployment and poverty, on the general wellness of students in dealing with financial challenges and constraints.

Financial needs and challenges of students

South Africa has one of the world's highest levels of inequality (NPC 2011: 3). Great poverty and great wealth co-exist side by side. It is therefore of the utmost importance that we actively create every opportunity to ensure that many more of those who currently or historically suffered from poverty and disadvantage are assisted to participate in the higher education sector. This is one of the main challenges for student affairs practitioners. For a majority of students, access and success are closely connected to the issue of finances. For the students to be accepted into university is just the first hurdle. Financial difficulty is seen as one of the key factors contributing to student attrition in South Africa, together with under-preparedness for higher education (Cosser & Letseka 2010: 3). In his foreword to the Student Housing Report, the minister of higher education and training emphasises the fact that '[M]any of our students, particularly those studying in our historically black institutions, have been living in very poor conditions and this has often hampered their ability to succeed' (DHET 2011: xi).

Despite the fact that the National Students Financial Aid Scheme (NSFAS) has been instrumental in increasing access for students who would otherwise have had no hope of obtaining tertiary education by providing financial aid to 659 000 students and distributing more than R12 billion in the first decade of its existence, the challenge has not been completely met (DHET 2010: 111). A number of academically deserving and financially needy students seem to be 'falling through the cracks of the scheme's bureaucracy', with the DHET recognising that there may be a 'bunching of students just beyond the cut-off point' (Letseka, Breier & Visser 2010: 38). The decades of discriminatory provision under apartheid continue to haunt the education system, affecting the chances and success of black, particularly poor, students (Letseka, Breier & Visser 2010: 25). It is a tragic fact that many students, mainly black, drop out of university every year without a qualification and huge debt – in other words, worse off and poorer, and also ashamed to even return to their hometowns because they have not been successful. There are, of course, many reasons for this unacceptable situation. Part of the problem has to do with the fact that many of these students only have bursaries and loans as a source of finances for their studies, and in many cases the bursaries do not cover all the costs of studying, leaving them struggling to cope. They came to university hoping that tertiary education would set them free from the poverty they have known all their life, only to leave the university disillusioned, with broken spirits.

Firfirey and Carolissen (2010) point out how students use multiple strategies to disguise their poverty from others – they are literally being silenced by the stigma of poverty, with feelings of hopelessness, while at the same time aggravating the harsh burden that they carry. They internalise oppression and resign themselves to accepting it (2010: 995). If bursaries or loans do not cover all the costs of studying, many students struggle to buy class notes (readers), pay for transport to service learning sites, and consequently find it extremely difficult to remain in the system and be successful in their studies. Firfirey and Carolissen (2010: 1000) therefore argue for an inclusive fee structure with minimal additional costs for the student's own pocket.

Student affairs practitioners see and know these ugly faces of poverty more than others on campus do. Many students feel safe enough to visit the offices of these practitioners. In many universities student affairs divisions have instituted various ways and means to at least alleviate the burden of financially challenged students through work-study programmes, assistantships and monthly supplies of basic toiletry items. Student affairs practitioners should continue to advocate a holistic integrated approach to student support and development. They are strategically well positioned to understand and appreciate the position of students and their struggles, and should therefore be the interpreters and advocates of student life and student issues. This implies an awareness that the six areas of wellness of students should be kept in mind, namely physical, spiritual, social, emotional, intellectual and occupational in a holistic, integrated and systemic approach (Cilliers 2008).

One way to ensure that their voice and the voices of students would be heard and taken seriously is to cultivate and develop strong ethical leadership among professionals and practitioners, as well as student leaders, increasing the credibility of the sector. Within the context of our current socio-political climate this is an extremely important part of restoring the moral fibre of the country and increasing confidence in leaders.

Cultivating and developing ethical leadership

Good student affairs practice provides opportunities for students, faculty staff, and student affairs educators to demonstrate the values that define a learning community. Effective learning communities are committed to justice, honesty, equality, civility, freedom, dignity, and responsible citizenship. Such communities challenge students to develop meaningful values for a life of learning. Standards espoused by student affairs divisions should reflect the values that bind the campus community to its educational mission (ACPA & NASPA 1997).

It is important for us to not only focus on ethical leadership for and among students, but we also need to live and demonstrate ethical values in our own work and life. Learning indeed has a moral context and it is expected of an educated person 'to possess certain traits of character, including the moral obligation to the common good' (Dalton, 1999: 45). The national context dictates that we raise the importance of a focus on ethical leadership. The national government's moral regeneration initiative has apparently come to a complete halt in some areas and so has the Western Cape joint initiative on ethical leadership. At the same time, levels of corruption have reached alarmingly high proportions, with obvious negative effects on the state's service delivery capacities. Many other social ills could be ascribed to the deterioration of ethical values and, furthermore, a worrying general attitude of 'Everyone is doing it' and 'I've got to look out for myself' has become part of a general culture among people. The common good has too often made way for self-interest and self-oriented materialistic values. Although corruption is not just a post-1994 phenomenon in South Africa, we concur with the NDP in its insistence that there can be no excuses for corruption today (NPC 2011: 401). The NDP's vision is 'a South Africa which has zero tolerance for corruption, in which an empowered citizenry have the confidence and knowledge to hold public and private officials to account and in which leaders hold themselves to high ethical standards and act with integrity' (NPC 2011: 402).

I believe universities are well-placed to – and should – take the lead to cultivate and develop ethical values in student leaders, preparing them to be change agents in society. Tertiary institutions occupy a position of privilege in society and it is not wrong that people expect high moral values from staff and students.

Dalton (1999: 51) suggests four 'inescapable areas' of student affairs practice that should help students to develop coherent moral values and ethical standards, namely 'learn and practice academic integrity; live responsibly in the community; develop citizenship skills and commitment for life after college; and grow and learn from personal moral crises and ethical conflicts'. A supporting community can contribute substantially to the development of students' values. Institutions should therefore be very clear regarding the values that they stand for. When students are confronted and challenged by the values and lifestyles of others, this encourages 'and even demand[s] reflectiveness and re-examination' of what they may know and believe (Dalton 1999: 55).

The way forward

The student affairs department within an institution committed to student learning and personal development should, according to *The Student Learning Imperative* (American College Personnel Association 1996), exhibit the following characteristics:

1. The student affairs department's mission complements the institution's mission, with the enhancement of student learning and personal development being the primary goal of student affairs programmes and services;
2. Resources are allocated to encourage student learning and personal development; and
3. Student affairs professionals collaborate with other institutional agents and agencies to promote student learning and personal development.

As learning is increasingly defined as more than classroom knowledge acquisition, student affairs units can claim a role in student learning that is neither peripheral nor optional. Student affairs can and should play an essential role 'by creating and maintaining a learning environment that fosters and maximizes student learning' (Hamrick, Evans & Shuh 2002: 126). This indeed has implications for restructuring student affairs practice and for preparing student affairs professionals and practitioners to play their crucial role in assuring highly educated and trained graduates who will be able to participate in the knowledge-driven economy of the future.

Some of the critical issues that were not discussed in this paper and which seem to be on the agenda at universities these days are the question of identity and culture, and the race issue. There are also questions around gender, sexuality and sexual practices that have to be debated in our multi-cultural society. Conversations around HIV/Aids, internationalisation and xenophobia, should also form part of programmes and agendas. Student affairs professionals and practitioners cannot withdraw from these conversations, but should rather create safe spaces and forums to encourage discussion.

Note

1. Partners involved in the Association of College and University Housing Officers-International South Africa Chapter (ACUHO-I SAC), Financial Aid Practitioners of South Africa (FAPSA), Higher Education Disability Services Association (HEDSA), National Association of Student Development Officers (NASDEV), the Southern Africa Association of Senior Student Affairs Professionals (SAASSAP), the Southern African Association for Counselling and Development in Higher Education (SAACDHE) and the South African Association of Campus Health Services (SAACHS).

Academic development: Bridging the gap for student development and success

Martin Mandew
Durban University of Technology

Summary

The various sectors working in the higher education system in general and in institutions of higher education in particular are, ostensibly, all working towards the same outcome, namely student success. But often there is no deep insight into or informed appreciation of each others' respective fields and of the efforts expended in pursuance of a common objective. The result is that the potential for structured collaboration and systematic cooperation for the benefit of the student is often not realised. This paper attempts to provide student affairs practitioners with a deeper insight into the *raison d'être* of 'academic development' (AD) as a field, viz. grappling with issues of teaching, learning and the curriculum. It sketches the development of AD as a field, its efforts to define and refine its mission, its struggle to re-invent itself, and other challenges it has had to contend with along the way. The paper highlights the critical carry-over issues and common student development and student success questions and argues for the exploration of a cross-cutting episteme.

Introduction

One of the fundamental challenges facing the higher education system in South Africa is the issue of *access*, *retention* and *success* of a large number of students from educationally disadvantaged backgrounds. The problem is complex and multi-layered and the academic development[1] movement has been grappling with it for at least the past 25 years. The problem has its origins in the apartheid policy in general and in its education policies in particular. These policies provided for separate, segregated and inferior education at both the pre-university and university levels for African, Coloured and Indian South Africans (collectively called Black), with Africans being the most deprived, not only materially but also epistemologically, that is, in terms of knowledge and skills equity. In contrast, the White education system was afforded the bulk of the financial resources, the best-qualified human capital and the best facilities and infrastructure, making it materially privileged and epistemologically advantaged.

Though a section of student affairs practitioners is directly involved in student development programmes, often, for many of the practitioners in the field, conceiving in a vivid, critical and theoretical manner of their own particular areas of work as related to the students' academic performance and success is not an easy exercise. Of course, there is an implicit and common sense intuition that all personnel employed by higher education institutions, whatever their responsibility or rank, somehow contribute to the institution's objectives and valued outcomes. This paper is intended to open wider the window into the academic sphere and shine a light on the academic challenges faced by educationally and socially disadvantaged students. It explores how higher education institutions have sought to deal with these challenges through interventions such as the AD programme in its various incarnations. The paper also discusses how the post-apartheid state has sought to both buttress and direct these interventions. Finally, the paper makes connections to student affairs, proposes an agenda for collaboration with academic development with a view to developing a common body of knowledge, and outlines critical issues and challenges that the student affairs movement in South Africa needs to attend to urgently for the sake of its own development and for the benefit of the students. Our primary interlocutors are therefore academic development and student affairs practitioners.

Towards a dialogical relationship

The *raison d'être* of student affairs and the primary role of its functionaries is to provide services and support and to develop and guide students towards success as they forge their way academically through the maze that is higher education (Mandew 2003: 61). It is hoped that through a better understanding of the academic challenges faced by students, and the ensuing AD initiatives and efforts, student affairs practitioners will be in a better position to rethink their own philosophy, re-examine their practice and review their strategies with a view to adding theoretical, practical and developmental value to student experience, academic success and holistic development endeavours. Furthermore, it is hoped that this will facilitate the beginning of a constructive dialogue between the AD field and the field of student affairs in exploring a common epistemology as they grapple with the following complex and critical questions:

- Who is the student?
- What do student development and student success entail?
- How is the interface between 'development' and 'success' constituted?
- What do the answers to the preceding questions imply for academic development and student affairs practice?

These questions are not exhaustive nor are they meant to be an end in themselves. They are intended to initiate a constructive dialogue that will facilitate a critical reflection on how together we can develop a common body of knowledge and make a positive and lasting impact on the development of the student.

What is 'academic development'?

As with many concepts, the term 'academic development' can mean different things depending on context and intent. For instance, in South Africa the term is also used in a more general sense to refer to all academic personnel 'doing developmental work in higher education institutions' (Volbrecht & Boughey 2004: 58). But this is not quite how we use the concept here. We employ it in a much more focused or specialised manner in two very closely related senses. In the first instance, we use it to denote the broad field or overarching discipline constituted of deliberate and structured interventions in the areas of *learning, teaching* and the *curriculum* initiated by higher education institutions to assist specifically students from educationally disadvantaged backgrounds to enter, cope and succeed at university. Volbrecht and Boughey define academic development as 'an open set of practices concerned with improving the quality of teaching and learning in higher education' (2004: 58).

Put differently, we use the overarching concept of academic development to refer to a structured and integrated process of raising the standard and improving the levels of the interrelated and mutually influencing *staff development*, *student development*[2] and *curriculum development* activities designed to facilitate student access and success in higher education. In the second instance, we use the term academic development in a much 'narrower' sense to refer to a specific trend, approach, or moment[3] in the evolution of the overarching discipline of AD. We discuss this trend or approach below under the heading *'Coming in from the cold?'*

Unpacking 'disadvantage'

We have noted that AD is essentially an intervention designed to mitigate and overcome the adverse impact of a disadvantaged social and educational background so that the student can *enter* university *and* succeed. Let us take a closer look at the notion of 'disadvantage' before we consider responses to it. Student affairs practitioners are *au fait* with the affective, non-academic and socio-environmental factors impacting on students from educationally and socially disadvantaged backgrounds as they navigate their way through the morass that is the higher education system. The students have to overcome a myriad of barriers such as the problem of hunger that many of them have to contend with on a daily basis, the inadequacy and unavailability of suitable housing and the problems associated with this and the perennial problem of a lack of finances despite the existence of the National Student Financial Aid Scheme. The unending emotional stress resulting from this plethora of problems that takes its toll on students, impacting on their ability to succeed. Many students, through no fault of their own, become casualties of the higher education system, as can be evidenced from the inordinately high attrition and low throughput rates[4], with financial indebtedness the only evidence that they 'have been' to university. These adverse environmental factors manifest but one dimension of disadvantage.

Much is made of the Matric or National Senior Certificate results (at the end of twelve years of general education), but the brutal truth is that these results are generally not a true reflection of student ability in that they cannot be used as a completely reliable predictor of student potential to cope and succeed at university[5]. This can generally be ascribed to the 'mismatch between the outcomes of schooling and the demands of the entry level [and even beyond] of higher education programmes' (Scott *et al.* 2007: 43). It is especially the case with respect to former Department of Education and Training (historically black) schools results. What this means in essence is that a student with an 'exemption' or 'bachelor' pass, which theoretically qualifies them to enter university, might not necessarily cope with the demands of higher learning, while a student whose results reflect a 'lower' pass might, with the necessary support and guidance, be able to cope and succeed at university. For this reason, many higher education institutions have over the years developed their own entrance tests or adopted the

National Benchmark Tests (NBT) as additional and fundamentally much more reliable gate-keeping mechanisms[6].

The 'educational disadvantage' or 'underpreparedness' means that students 'have generally not been exposed to key academic approaches and experiences taken for granted in traditional higher education programmes' (Scott et al. 2007: 42), resulting in an educational 'gap' or 'deficit'. This manifests in the lack of certain complex proficiencies that are required in order to succeed at university, viz. cognitive skills, communication and academic language skills, subject content, attitudes to learning and life skills (Grayson 1997; Scott et al. 2007; Kloot et al. 2008)[7]. An often cited expression of underpreparedness on the part of these students is said to be their proclivity for rote-learning. In essence, rote-learning is learning and memorising without deep comprehension and internalised understanding and it is totally unsuited and inadequate for successfully engaging the demands of higher education.

Deficient Others

The origins of AD can be traced back to the late 1970s and early 1980s[8] when the four English-speaking, historically White, liberal universities (Rhodes, Natal, Cape Town and Witwatersrand) began to admit a small number of Black students from educationally disadvantaged schools (Volbrecht & Boughey 2004; Boughey 2007, 2010) as a result of a relaxation in apartheid policies (Pavlich & Orkin, cited in Boughey 2010)[9]. These early initiatives were known as academic support programmes (ASP) and represent the first trend or thrust in AD efforts. A key feature of the ASPs was their focus on overcoming factors of underpreparedness or disadvantage inherent to the individual student. From an ideological point of view, ASPs were primarily concerned with issues of equity (non-discrimination) and equality (Boughey 2007). As Boughey (2010: 5) puts it:

> Early initiatives were therefore inherently liberal in intent in that they focused on attempting to give Black students 'equal opportunity' by filling the gap between their poor socio-economic and educational backgrounds and university.

In truth and practice, though, when these students were admitted to the liberal universities they were viewed as 'deficient Others'. They were *different* and were found *wanting*. They did not fit the dominant demographic profile of these institutions and lacked what it takes to succeed academically. As such, they required a lot of remedial work in order for them to fit and be assimilated into a well-established, self-satisfied immutable system. It is safe to say that from the perspective of the liberal intent of these institutions, these 'deficient Others' would always be welcome but it was assumed they would continue to constitute a minority into the foreseeable future. ASP staff were primarily teachers and language specialists as opposed to 'being academics'. They were appointed on short-term contract on the basis of their teaching expertise and experience, with no real prospects for permanent employment or tenure. The posts they occupied were often funded with soft money sourced externally rather than from within the universities' own financial resources, indicating in no uncertain terms that the problem was really someone else's.

A key priority of ASPs was the issue of *access,* that is, mechanisms of bringing the students into the system. It was crucial to identify students who, despite poor Matric results and a disadvantaged schooling system, had the potential to cope with the demands of university and ultimately succeed, that is, graduate. For this reason, a great deal of work was done to develop mechanisms to test and assess 'potential' which was later refined to assessing minimum proficiency, basic reasoning skills, synthesis and logical deduction ability, basic comprehension capability, grammar and syntax (Grussendorff *et al.* 2004). The use of these well-developed and refined entry tests still continues to this day (Boughey 2010: 5).

ASP initially dealt with the problem of 'disadvantage' in an intuitive fashion, drawing on popular rather than mainly academic sources. ASPs provided additional classes and tutorials and special courses in language and study skills (Volbrecht & Boughey 2004; Boughey 2007, 2010). The ASP solution was largely language-proficiency driven and what little academic theory was drawn upon was based largely on the discipline of applied linguistics and emanated from outside South Africa, with little consideration of the local socio-cultural and political context and educational complexities (Volbrecht & Boughey 2004). These early interventions were conceived and thought of as 'bridging' programmes designed to 'fill the gaps' existing in the knowledge of the students coming out of educationally disadvantaged backgrounds (Kloot *et al.* 2008).

In spite of their good intentions, the early ASP initiatives were not necessarily popular with the students for whom they were intended. This is understandable because they were offered in addition to the normal first year courses students were taking. This meant that the burden on students who were already struggling was enormous, if not unbearable. Moreover, the ASP tutorials and classes were not credit-bearing and as such students were not particularly motivated to participate in or commit themselves to attending the sessions on a regular basis. Some students cynically referred to them as 'African Support Programmes'.

ASP work was located physically, financially, intellectually, ideologically and academically *outside* the academic mainstream of institutions, thus completing and institutionalising Othering[10]. In true liberal form, this was not a purely racialised form of Othering aimed at educationally disadvantage Black students. It had an equally strong sexist component, targeting AD tutors and personnel, most of whom were White women, excluding them not only from the mainstream academic and intellectual sphere but also materially from the remuneration and reward system of the university. The message was clear and unambiguous: 'You are not one of us. You are less than us. Therefore you deserve less than us'.

Coming in from the cold

With the sweeping and radical changes in the socio-political environment that began in the late 1980s, culminating in the negotiated political settlement in 1994, it was self-evident and inevitable that the higher education field would be in for major changes – structurally, systemically and ideologically, a process referred to as *transformation*. This period saw the emergence of a new trend or thrust that sought to be fundamentally different, philosophically more radical, conceptually more advanced, educationally more sound, practically more challenging and was inevitably financially more demanding than the ASP model.

In essence, the new thrust sought to de-ghettoise the earlier intervention strategy and the name was formally changed from 'academic support' to 'academic/ education development'. It was envisaged that this would be a complete departure from the ASP model. It sought to effect a fundamental and systemic change by mainstreaming AD, i.e. putting AD at the centre of faculties and departmental activities. Tinkering at the edges would no longer do[11]. This new thrust would also be known as the 'infusion' model (Walker & Badsha 1993). Put differently, it sought to be a method of 'adding in' rather than 'adding on'. But what would this new approach entail at a philosophical and practical level?

At the level of the institution one of the significant steps that were taken to institutionalise the new approach was to avail resources for the establishment of central hubs or units whose main task was to be the engine for driving, directing and coordinating campus-wide activities of planting, growing and nurturing AD *inside* faculties and departments. Some AD specialists were then placed in departments and faculties, at the coalface of academic activities as it were, to 'play a role in curriculum and staff development' (Volbrecht & Boughey 2004: 63).

The new approach sought to engender a shift from the individualised deficit model that located the problem in the individual student, to debunking dominant assumptions about what it means to be an academic at a university. In the words of Moulder (1991):

> Academics are employed to teach *all* students who register for a course. They aren't employed to teach only those students who have the knowledge and skills they would like them to have. *[emphasis added]*

There was a view that sought to move away from the deficit model to one that recognised that students from educationally disadvantaged backgrounds drew from different forms of cultural capital to those of their mainstream white counterparts (Mandew 1993). At the level of the curriculum, there were renewed and novel approaches to addressing the issue of 'language development' to being something deeper and more critical than the earlier simplistic diagnosis of the problem as being one of 'English' as a second, third, or even fourth language. The new approach would be one of *language across the curriculum*, proposing the solution as (i) a broad one of *academic literacy*: and (ii) using language experts based in the AD Centre to work with staff in departments 'so that language and literacy was developed in mainstream lectures and through mainstream assignments' (Boughey 2005: 29).

In order to buttress the language development efforts, 'writing centres' were established, aimed at both students and staff. For the student, the writing centres sought to develop their academic writing skills, while they provided support to staff as well so that a 'common cause of writing development' between staff and student could be promoted (Leibowitz & Parkerson in Boughey 2005). Other elements of the infusion model entailed language policy development, materials development, developing appropriate assessment methods, learning theory, research skills training, developing tutorials to be embedded in mainstream academic work, supplemental instruction programmes[12], tutor training, learning resources such as transformed and transformative computer-supported learning, developing effective student selection methods, student residences-based peer-group learning projects, and student participation at AD association conferences (Walker & Badsha 1993). The infusion model was very ambitious in both its conceptualisation and objective but it has not been the only AD show in town. It has co-existed with an equally formidable and increasingly popular approach.

Building firm foundations

Another key AD intervention was the strategy of introducing foundation programmes, initially in the natural sciences stream, and later in the human sciences. Essentially, foundation courses are conceptualised as *access and retention* programmes. They are designed to facilitate entry into and success at university. The historically white institutions were the first to go this route[13]. The foundation courses were initially largely externally funded[14]. Some historically black institutions followed suit because for them the problem was even bigger in that it was not a minority, but a majority of their student intake that was 'underprepared'[15]. Of course, with the changes in the socio-political environment, the historically white institutions were also to be faced with the imperative of having to admit a large number of black students, many being 'underprepared' and coming from former DET schools. Over the years, some institutions have acquired good reputations for running and consistently improving what are considered to be flagship foundation programmes.

Conceptually, foundation programmes can be considered to be different from 'bridging' programmes. The latter 'assume that the students are at a level close to what is needed for university work, and then attempt to provide an intermediate stepping stone between school and university' (Grayson 1996: 993). Another way of distinguishing 'bridging' programmes is that they 'attempt to look back to the Senior Certificate syllabus which is then retaught in an attempt to improve students' readiness to engage with tertiary studies' (Boughey 2005: 13). As the name suggests, foundation programmes have been designed to 'lay the foundations' for the 'underprepared student' on which to build the knowledge, capabilities, skills and self-confidence required for the acquisition of a university qualification. Rather than looking backwards to the Senior Certificate syllabus, foundation courses look forward to the university curriculum and endeavour to impart the capabilities and concepts that are required as a foundation for further learning (Boughey 2005). Satisfactory performance at foundation level is required for students to proceed into the mainstream or on to the next level.

Three key features common to most foundation-type programmes are that (i) there is a credit-bearing element embedded in them that count towards the qualification; (ii) there is an additional year built into the acquisition of the qualification (also referred to as 'extended' or 'augmented' programmes)[16]; and (iii) though there are differentials with regard to entry levels between foundation students and regular students, the exit standards and learning outcomes are said to be demonstrably on par for both foundational and direct-access cohorts.

Though it has had strong elements of trial-and-error, the design, construction and implementation of foundation programmes has not been a haphazard affair. To a large extent it has been a meticulous and carefully considered process that has been shaped by sound educational principles and rigorous pedagogical processes aimed at illuminating issues around subject matter and the structuring of instructional activities. It has been informed by complex theories explicating the role of the learner, the role of the teacher, and how the learning process occurs (Grayson 1996). The theories employed in the development of foundational courses have variously drawn from the frameworks of cognitive psychology such as constructivism and from social theory. Constructivism focuses on the individualised aspects of learning, stressing that, fundamentally, learning is a process that occurs and is constructed *within the individual* (intrapsychologically), whereas social theories stress that learning is fundamentally and primarily a process that is socio-culturally mediated (interpsychologically)[17] (Grayson 1996; Volbrecht & Boughey 2004; Downs 2005).

In general, foundation courses have been constituted of the following package of knowledge, capabilities and skills development designed to provide epistemological and vocational access: integrated degree-specific disciplines, i.e. knowledge of subject content; vocational skills, i.e. insight into the thinking and behaviour required in a specific profession[18]; integration and transfer skills, i.e. the use and relation of concepts and learnings between cognate disciplines and contexts; knowledge-construction skills, i.e. the ability to construct knowledge and meaning based (i) on experimentation and observation of natural phenomena and (ii) on reflecting on and analysis of cogent ideas and coherent views; academic literacy and communication skills, i.e. understanding and use of discipline-specific language and conventions; reasoning and problem-solving skills; metacognitive skills, i.e. learning-about-learning (the awareness of and control over one's own process of learning and understanding in a reflective and conscious manner); practical skills, viz. laboratory-related and computer-related; group-learning skills; life skills, eg study skills, coping skills, time-management, conflict resolution, etc. Of course, not all foundation programmes necessarily lay claim to this comprehensive catalogue of knowledge and skills development. Also, the nomenclature between institutions, programmes and qualifications might not be uniform but the underlying skills-concepts and outcomes envisaged are broadly equivalent, viz. the development of higher-order thinking skills. But have these foundation programmes succeeded in achieving the desired outcomes, in terms of facilitating equity of access and enabling equity of success?

Hitting the sweet spot

As can be expected, the adoption and implementation of foundation programmes has hardly been a walk in the park. An obviously central and critical question that has been raised is whether it is really possible to overcome twelve years of effective under-preparation in one year of foundational courses. A formal assessment of student performance in one of the Science Foundation Programme (SFP) courses confirms that one year is definitely not sufficient[19]. The investigation came to the conclusion 'that the skills required for more theoretical tasks need ongoing practice and development over a sustained period [and that] this would need to be continued into the mainstream courses if students were to improve' (Downs 2005: 667). The issue of the inadequacy of one year points to the need to embed AD in mainstream courses as espoused in the infusion model. It underscores the issue of 'more time and more tuition' (Kloot *et al.* 2008) as a *sine qua non* for all effective interventions.

These shortcomings and weaknesses notwithstanding, evidence indicates that there is an inherent educational benefit in the foundation programmes in enhancing and empowering students as active participants in the process of learning and in encouraging deep learning (Downs 2005: 679). Results of assessments undertaken so far indicate that, despite some challenges, the impact and efficacy of the foundation programmes is overwhelmingly positive and very encouraging. For example, in terms of the overall impact, the SFP at the University of KwaZulu-Natal 'has made a significant contribution to increasing the number of Black African students at the tertiary level, particularly in the Faculty of Science and Agriculture' (Downs 2010: 102). In terms of the time taken to complete the qualification, SFP students were 'generally equivalent to or better than other mainstream science students and approached minimum time' (Southway-Ajulu in Downs 2010: 103). A number of these SFP graduates have proceeded and succeeded at Masters level, with a few also completing doctoral degrees. Interestingly and worthy of noting, the 'SFP has significantly increased black women participation in the [natural] sciences' (Downs 2010: 106).

The SFP at the University of Limpopo indicates equally positive outcomes. Students who have gone through this foundation programme have consistently performed better than direct access students and also better than those direct students who have repeated a level at year one and marginally higher in subsequent years of the degree (Zaaiman 1998 and Letsoalo 2001 in Mabila *et al.* 2006)[20].

A study conducted into a human sciences foundation programme, also makes significant and positive findings on the efficacy of the programme[21]. The study concludes that students who went through the programme 'had significantly higher graduation rates than mainstream students (African, Coloured and Indian students) and lower drop-out rates and exclusions', were on par with White students, and there was no difference between these students and mainstream students in the time taken to complete the degree (Tyson 2010: 114–115).

A longitudinal study conducted into a foundation programme at the Nelson Mandela Metropolitan University makes equally encouraging findings. It concludes that the foundation students 'tend to perform better in later degree studies than directly admitted students with similar academic profiles' (Wood & Lithauer 2005: 1002). In addition, reflecting on their experience of the foundation programme, these students attest to receiving benefits beyond the academic sphere, viz. the development of self-knowledge, an improved sense of self-worth, development of self-management skills, improvement in attitude, improved communication skills, and the formation of support systems (Wood & Lithauer 2005).

Are we there yet?

At a systemic and structural level, what AD in general and foundation programmes in particular have done is to directly or indirectly compel institutions to begin the unsettling and inconvenient process of rethinking their assumptions about two critical and related questions. The process is unsettling because it suggests that it cannot be business as usual in thinking about the *purpose* of higher education. It is inconvenient because it implies thinking in new ways about the *process* of the business of higher education. The two critical and related questions are: (i) 'Who is the student?' socially, economically, politically, culturally, educationally, etc.; and (ii) 'How prepared is the institution for who the student is in the way that it is currently defining, structuring, configuring and offering its academic programmes?' As a result, institutions have had to, *mutatis mutandis*, diversify and nuance their entry level assumptions and rethink both the teaching and the configuration of their qualifications, allowing for flexibility and for a diversity of valid and effective approaches to the same qualification to co-exist.

But are these responses adequate and sufficiently deep? Are the answers to the first critical question revealing anything new or is the student still viewed as '*deficient*' or as '*the Other*', or still as both: '*the deficient Other*'? If not, then who *is* the student? In terms of the second critical question, philosophically and practically, how have mainstream curricular conceptualisations, programme constructions, pedagogical approaches, programme management structures and research agenda been impacted upon? Has a new consciousness and practice emerged in respect of what it means to be an academic vis-à-vis Moulder's earlier assertion? How is the relationship between the academic (discipline-specialist) and the AD expert constituted? How is engagement between them structured and facilitated? What is the nature and manifestation of power in this relationship between the discipline expert and the AD expert? What role does power play in the structuring and facilitation of the engagement? Where and how does the student feature in the scheme of things? Is the student at the centre or at the margins? At the policy, management and strategic level the question that has been raised by Volbrecht and Boughey (2004: 57) is how are the previously fragmented communities and fields of knowledge/practice to be integrated?

A criticism of foundation programmes is that, generally, the class sizes have tended to be relatively small in numbers with the result that systemically, the impact has been rather limited, the critical mass in terms of throughput rates has not been achieved and, systemically, the ripple effect has largely not happened. Put differently, the argument is that the foundational programmes have managed to level only a relatively small patch of the playing field.

Put your money where your mouth is

A key issue that has acted as a constraint in AD has been the issue of funding. We saw that for a considerable period many of the programmes were funded largely through soft money, sourced from outside government and outside higher education institutions. This constraint has had far-reaching consequences in several respects. Key among these has been the issue of the professionalisation of AD staff in terms of academic qualifications, and the generation of knowledge in the field. We noted that AD staff were 'low-level' staff in terms of academic qualifications, and were appointed on short-term contract basis. As a result, they were denied easy access to institutional resources to improve their qualifications as AD practitioners. Also, they did not have the wherewithal to conduct much-needed research into AD practice and issues, thus constraining development of capacity in the field (Boughey 2010). Many of the AD practitioners were graduate students who were pursuing 'pure' qualifications in mainstream fields rather than AD-related qualifications. These constraints notwithstanding, some practitioners in the field have soldiered on admirably, overcoming structural, systemic and other constraints, generating phenomenal knowledge in the AD discipline while also developing formidable expertise in the field.

Over the years, the government has taken note of the success, though limited, of AD interventions and of pockets of excellence and relative success, especially foundation-type programmes, and has recognised their potential systemic impact. The 1997 White Paper entitled *A Programme for the Transformation of Higher Education* and the 2001 *National Plan for Higher Education* specifically recognised the role of foundational courses and extended programmes and the impact they could make. The new higher education funding framework of 2003 made provision to fund extended curriculum programmes. These earmarked funds were given in three tranches covering the years 2007/2008, 2008/2009 and 2009/2010. This has led to more institutions introducing foundation programmes. In 2010 there were 45 foundation-type access programmes in South Africa (Downs 2010: 98). What does the proliferation of these types of programmes suggest for the higher education system in South Africa? Are they to be considered a stop-gap measure to mitigate against a weak general education system, or are they the future?

Critical questions for the student affairs movement

As student affairs practitioners, what lessons can we learn from the struggles, setbacks and victories AD movement? As the recent Physics Education Review indicates, under-preparation in the General Education system is continuing unabated (SAIP 2013)[22]. The problem of articulation between the general/further education system and the higher education system is going to be with us for a while yet. In short, challenges relating to access and success are not about to disappear any time soon. There is, however, much that can be done to improve the preparedness of the higher education system to develop students and engender student success. For the student affairs movement, the obvious place to begin is with our own preparedness in terms of our capacity and capabilities as producers of critical student affairs knowledge for the South African context. The recurring refrain one hears from student affairs practitioners is that very little has been written about the field in South Africa. This may be true. But what are the reasons for this? Many practitioners feel inadequate in terms of the skills required to be knowledge producers in respect of student affairs issues. As with other skills, knowledge production skills are learnt, developed and honed with practice – over time. There is no better place than the university to acquire, develop and perfect these skills. An obvious strategic objective would be to partner with the AD movement to equip student affairs practitioners with knowledge production skills specific for their field.

Linked to the academic development of student affairs practitioners is the need to map out student affairs issues to be explored and questions to be investigated for purposes of the proposed knowledge production endeavour. As student affairs practitioners, we must intensify the difficult task of grappling with the key issues and critical questions pertaining to the imperatives of the preparedness of the higher education system in general and our own preparedness in particular. Of course, it is much easier to go abroad to do benchmarking and to import externally developed solutions with a view to adapting them for our situation and context. Without detracting from the inherent value of benchmarking, the question needs to be asked, however: to what extent are these 'adapted solutions' derived from 'developed' countries appropriate for our context? Is student affairs practice in South African in a state of inertia or are we on top of our game? Only South African student affairs practitioners can produce the critical knowledge required for *their* field and context. The ideal moment to do this will never arrive. It is up to us to create conditions for this ideal moment. It is incumbent on the disparate student affairs organisations therefore to come together to draw up and implement a long term strategic plan for the development of the student affairs field as a knowledge-production field for our context. Student affairs practitioners need to develop a kindred spirit with their AD counterparts for the benefit of the student. Apart from human and financial resources this task requires vision, commitment and leadership.

Another area that merits attention is the field of student development programmes. Currently, each institution designs its own student development programme with little if any collaboration with other institutions. As student affairs, do we have a common and shared vision for student development and student success? Have any of the current student development programmes offered by student affairs been rigorously evaluated? Are these programmes coherently structured? Are they effective? How can they be improved? Do the programmes reach all the students? Can these programmes be sufficiently developed to be credit-bearing and/or be registered on the qualifications framework? Can we as the student affairs movement agree on an inter-disciplinary research agenda with our AD colleagues to jointly seek answers to some of the complex questions relating to student development and student success? Some of the questions that need to be explored are: What does student development and student success mean and entail? Who is the student who enters our higher education system? Is the 'first-year-experience' the best it can be for students? How is it currently constituted? How can it be improved? Who is the student who exits the system prematurely? Who is the student who exits the system through graduation? What are his/her attributes? Are these attributes suitable and appropriate for the world of work? Are these attributes appropriate for democracy and responsible citizenship?

It is critical that student affairs practitioners think consciously, purposefully and systematically about their contribution to student development and student success. There is a need to pose probing questions about what it means to be a student affairs practitioner. It is incumbent on us to put the assumptions of our practice under the microscope and to subject them to a much closer examination and a more intense scrutiny. Are we as student affairs practitioners mere functionaries performing mechanical tasks and carrying out non-reflective actions, or are we able to define a much deeper and more fundamental purpose for our existence? In the South African context of higher education what is the philosophical glue that holds us together as the student affairs field? Who is defining and setting our agenda? What is the place and agenda of student affairs in the overall scheme of higher education? Are we focused on the task at hand? To what extent do power games such as institutional politics, divisional wranglings, personal ambitions, personality issues and inter-organisational suspicions detract us from the critical thoughts we should be thinking, the probing questions we should be asking, the vital answers we should be seeking and the important things we should be doing?

How do student affairs contribute to institutional preparedness in respect of our programmes, the various services we offer and the policies we formulate and implement? Have we rigorously evaluated the appropriateness of our services and the effectiveness of our support structures? To what extent are we engaged in Othering practices and policies? Are we employing existing resources effectively and efficiently? Again, how and where does the student feature? Is the voice of the student audible? Is this voice intelligible? Where do our weaknesses and strengths lie? What does student affairs preparedness mean in terms of intra-student affairs cooperation and inter-institutional collaboration? In short, as the student affairs movement, what do we need to do philosophically, strategically, developmentally, programmatically and practically to up the ante and take student development and student success to new and greater heights?

Conclusion

Fact is, the AD movement in South Africa has made great strides since its humble beginnings more than 25 years ago. It has had a huge and positive impact on higher education. This progress has not been accidental. It can be ascribed to a relentless struggle to grapple with the critical challenge of access and success. A key feature of this struggle has been the discipline and intellectual rigour that practitioners, despite marginalisation, have applied in reflecting on their practice and mission. The body of knowledge and expertise that the movement has generated is phenomenal. In its turn, student affairs in South Africa is arguably as old as the university and has largely played a supportive role that has not always demanded critical, rigorous and intellectual reflection on practice and mission. Needless to say, these days are long gone and the student affairs movement also has to contend with issues of access, student development and success and reflect these in its practice, programmes, services and policy choices. We have proposed the questions to be explored in this regard and suggested synergistic collaboration with the academic development movement as a possible way forward.

Notes

1. In other contexts, 'academic development' (AD) is known as 'educational development'.
2. This refers specifically to student academic development as opposed to 'general' or 'holistic' student development as generally employed and understood in the field of student affairs/services.
3. In her writings Boughey uses the term 'phases' as an analytical tool to denote distinction rather than to imply strictly sequential and discrete stages.
4. The issue of high attrition and low throughput rates is not a new phenomenon in South Africa. Studies conducted in the 1930s, 1950s and 1960s into White students' performance indicate very low throughput rates (Akojee & Nkomo 2007 in Kioko 2010). A 1963 study indicates a throughput rate of 55%, of which 49% were constituted of White males (Malherbe 1977 in Kioko 2010). Currently, the attrition rate at first year level is 40% of *all* students admitted at our universities with a cohort throughput rate of a mere 30% for a three year qualification over a five year period, with the graduation rate for Black students being less than that for White students in all fields of study (Scott *et al.* 2007).
5. The unpredictability of the NSC results is most pronounced in results from the former deprived apartheid Department of Education and Training schools (Hofmeyr & Spence 1989, Yeld & Haeck 1997 cited in Van der Flier *et al.* 2003).
6. National Benchmark Tests are designed to achieve three things: (i) to assess entry-level academic literacy and mathematics skills, (ii) to assess the relationship between entry-level skills and school-level exit results, and (iii) to provide institutions requiring additional information in the admission and placement of entry-level students.
7. There is a twist though to this 'under-prepared' discourse. In the view of Miller 'students from disadvantaged backgrounds may be over-prepared in the sense what impedes their progress at university is not new learning …but learning to unlearn' (cited in Mphahlele 1994: 50).
8. This was well before the momentous political changes which began with the release of political prisoners and the unbanning of anti-apartheid political movements in the early 1990s.
9. Strictly speaking, these were not the first attempts to admit Black students into White institutions. For example, the University of Natal had since the 1960s accepted Black students into its exclusively Black medical school and the University of the Witwatersrand had established a 'slow stream' programme in the 1970s (Mphahlele 1994: 49).
10. Though it has earlier origins, the notion of 'Othering' was first systematically employed and popularized by Gayatri Spivak in her groundbreaking essay 'The Rani of Sirmur' as an analytical tool to demonstrate how colonizers in India justified and institutionalised their power, moral superiority and monopoly of superior knowledge over the colonised, who they defined into existences as Others who were different from and, more importantly, inferior to them.
11. The University of the Western Cape came to epitomise this new approach. For a crisp and vivid exposition of this new vision of academic development see Walker & Badsha (1993).
12. *Supplemental instruction* was defined as being 'voluntary, non-remedial, student driven, cost effective and [focusing] on high-risk courses rather than high-risk students, and, most importantly, SI leaders [receiving] intensive training in the principles of non-directive facilitation of small groups' (Davies & Vorster 1994: 166 cited in Boughey 2005: 30).
13. The University of Cape Town introduced its Science Foundation Programme (SFP) in 1986 and the University of Natal (Pietermaritzburg) introduced its SFP in 1991, and its Humanities Access Programme in 2001, with the latter being internally funded. The Durban campus of the University of Natal had a four year BSc programme (referred to as the 'Augmented Programme') which admitted students directly into first-year course as early as 1991 (Kirby undated).
14. For instance, students participating in the SFP at the University of Natal (Pietermaritzburg) received bursaries from the United States Agency for International Development (Downs 2010: 105).

15. The University of the North's Science Foundation Year (UNIFY) was introduced in 1992 (Mabila *et al.* 2006: 295). The University has now been renamed the University of Limpopo. The University of Durban-Westville introduced it Science Foundation Programme in 1999 (Kirby undated).
16. There have been exceptions, though, such as at the School of Theology at the University of Natal (Pietermaritzburg) where there was no additional year (due to a combination of financial constraints and pedagogical considerations). The introduction of foundation courses brought about a complete reconceptualisation and reorganisation of the School's bachelor degree curriculum, with two foundation courses being introduced, one at first year level and the other at the second year level.
17. The foremost and frequently cited exponent of the social aspect theory of teaching and learning among AD practitioners has been Lev S Vygotsky (1896-1934), a Russian cognitive psychologist, who wrote the seminal book *Mind in Society: The Development of Higher Psychological Processes*. Two key ideas in the theory of Vygotsky are the notions of the 'zone of proximal development' (ZPD) and 'scaffolding'. The ZPD is the gap or interval between what the learner (adult or child) can learn on their own, and what they can learn with the assistance of a more experienced and knowledgeable person. In order for the learner to learn new concepts and skills, the knowledgeable person (teacher) must provide scaffolds to support the learning experience. These scaffolds are then removed when the required learning has occurred. (www.social.jrank.org)
18. Garraway (2010) argues that in the case of universities of technology which are essentially more vocation oriented, foundations courses have to begin the process of inducting the student into the vocation or profession of their field of study.
19. Undertaken at the University of KwaZulu-Natal, this study by CT Downs (2005) is aptly entitled: 'Is a year-long access course into university helping previously disadvantaged Black students in biology?'
20. For a detailed breakdown of the statistics see Mabila *et al.* (2006) and Downs (2010).
21. The study was undertaken as a master's degree investigation at the University of Natal. (Tyson 2010)
22. As the SAIP Review indicates, the issue of under-preparedness is not unique to South Africa but is a global phenomenon. However, 'the level of under-preparedness is *substantially worse* in South Africa than in almost all other countries' [original emphasis]. (2013: 14)

Student success as the number one affair in student affairs: A structural inequality outlook

Matete Madiba
University of Pretoria

Summary

This paper seeks to locate student success as a priority in the agenda of student affairs in South African higher education. The paper explores indicators of student success and argues that the quality of 'graduatedness', like all the other indicators, is as much a matter of the classroom as it is of organised student life outside the classroom. A further argument the paper makes is that student success is a useful point of departure to talk about an integrated and holistic development of students. The paper adopts the 'structural racism' framework of the Aspen Institute (2004) and appropriates the framework as 'structural inequality' to look at issues that affect student success in and outside the classroom. It argues that despite the publicly claimed mantra of redress, access and equity, many role-players in South African higher education, within and outside the academy, are perpetrators of structural inequality. Citing successful examples, it concludes that there is a need for a deliberate, concerted and collective effort by all role-players in order to achieve student success.

Introduction

As I set out to complete this paper, I could not avoid paying attention to the 'screams' in the reports on the crisis of the non-delivery of textbooks in Limpopo province. The *Mail & Guardian* (13–19 July 2012) reports on how 'the poor lose', and mentions amongst others that '47 per cent of the country's 12 million pupils are in schools that are funded at minimum levels' and that less than 1 per cent of grade nine learners met the requirement to get the weekly minimum of four language exercises in their curriculum. The article is based on data that exposes 'the staggering inequalities in the state of schooling' in South Africa and draws its data from the *National School Monitoring Survey* dated May 2012. The report paints a very dim future for the coming generations who will be entering higher education: a depressing context from which to reflect on student success in South African higher education, and on success indicators defined in terms of enrolment, graduation and throughput rates at this stage. The question we need to grapple with is how far are we in refining our tools, both conceptual and otherwise, to deal with these challenges? More poignantly, a critical question is how far are we going to perpetuate 'structural inequality' in the new South Africa?

It is this question on perpetuating 'structural inequality' that makes me turn to the work of the Aspen Institute in America for a framework that will allow me to look backward and forward in understanding the gains and losses we are making in student success in South African higher education. The Aspen Institute publication on *Structural Racism and community building* (2004) provides a critical lens through which to view the issues that threaten student success in this country. The Aspen Institute Roundtable on Community Change, formerly known as Aspen Institute Roundtable on Comprehensive Community Initiatives is a good example of the 'collective impact' strategy that receives a brief treatment later in this paper.

The publication moves from the premise that 'race and poverty are still strongly linked in America' and this is 40 years after African-Americans were allowed to vote. The report looks at the census data of 2000 and reveals that 'a person of color is nearly three times more likely to be poor than a white person'. The publication goes on to focus on a number of questions and argues that these questions matter, and further posits that 'white Americans remain significantly more likely than racial minorities to have access to what it takes to fulfill their inborn potential to succeed in life, and to be rewarded fairly for their efforts' (The Aspen Institute 2004). It is within this context that the publication makes the claim that 'effort to promote a just society and vibrant democracy is not likely to succeed without an honest and unflinching appraisal of the role that race plays in all of our lives.' The authors advance their argument in this way:

> Without fully accounting for the historical and ongoing ways in which racial dynamics produce inequities between whites and

people of color, the social justice and antipoverty field risks pursuing strategies that are misguided, incomplete, or inappropriate to the challenge. (The Aspen Institute 2004)

They go on to 'review how race shapes political, economic, and cultural life in the USA, and offer insights for integrating a racial equity perspective into the work of community building and socioeconomic justice.' I draw from the insights in the Aspen Institute publication and appropriate the integration of the equity perspective in looking at student success and student affairs in South African higher education. I also note that even though there are many parallels, what makes the South African context even more disturbing is that those that are at the receiving end of inequality are the majority and not the minority as in the USA. The authors use the term 'structural racism' to refer to 'a system in which public policies, institutional practices, cultural representations, and other norms work in various, often reinforcing ways to perpetuate racial group inequity'. Though I find the concept to resonate so much with what is happening in South Africa, I choose to replace 'racism' with 'inequity' and my appropriation of the concept results in the term 'structural inequality', which does not exclude but is not limited to racism.

The authors in the Aspen publication continue to point out that structural racism 'touches and implicates everyone in our society'. They make a revealing claim and stress that 'position and mobility within the racial hierarchy, which in some ways resembles a caste system, cannot be determined by the non-white or subordinated groups.' This claim says a lot in terms of understanding student success and the 'disadvantaged', that it is not necessarily within their power to determine a shift in the position they find themselves in. They are somehow structurally disarmed of their agency and a number of factors and role-players reinforce that state. Even more revealing is the point that how 'those who are at the lower end of the privilege scale perceive themselves, or how they behave, is less significant to their racial privilege status than broadly held perceptions about them.' At the centre of their thesis is the argument that 'structural racism' (to read as structural inequality in the thesis of this paper) provides a lens that 'allows us to see more clearly how our nation's core values – and the public policies and institutional practices that are built on them – perpetuate social stratifications and outcomes that all too often reflect racial group sorting rather than individual merit and effort.' I would like to argue that in the South African context, a lot of role-players that surround higher education are perpetrators of structural inequality, and there is a dire need for a critical look and a seizure of agency to make a contribution and to stop the perpetration. Student success is tightly linked to issues of equity, and at various levels different role players have to scrutinise their practices and identify how guilty they are of this charge, and find ways to rectify their actions. It is a moral issue.

Stock-taking in the South African context

The Green Paper (2011) summarises the challenges associated with student success so far and clearly articulates the current challenges facing the sector: low success and throughput rates. The case for low success and throughput was laid out earlier in the work done by Scott, Yeld and Hendry (2007). The Green Paper (2011: 41) points out that

> South African universities are characterised by relatively low success rates: 74 per cent in 2010, compared to a desired national norm of 80 per cent. This results in a graduation rate of 15 per cent – well below the national norm of 25 per cent for students in three-year degree programmes in contact education.

In the case that Scott *et al.* (2007) made, low participation rates are a significant part of the challenge faced by the sector. Citing the work by Cloete *et al.* (2002) they argued:

> Research in the area of access and equity has so far indicated that the expansion of the higher education system from 395 700 headcount enrolments in 1990 to 732 000 in 2005 has not necessarily meant a significant increase in the actual participation of African students in higher education.

The purpose of the research by Scott *et al.*, was to make a case for 'the quality of higher education graduates', adding the notion of quality to the suite of indicators in student success. This way of defining student success places focus on what institutions should be able to produce in the light of government targets and it is framed within the bigger outcomes of redress, access and equity. It also highlights the role of agency in addressing challenges within this environment. Moja and Hayward (2005) provide a critique in terms of how state agency was exercised, especially through funding, in the redress agenda in a period of 15 years linked to South African democracy. They draw a contrast between individual and institutional redress and argue that 'only limited institutional redress occurred' and the 'record is much better for individual redress' (Moja & Hayward 2005: 49). The contrast is both useful and interesting in that it draws attention to an elusive tension to deal with in student success and equity focused projects: state versus individual agency.

Luckett (2005) is critical of the 'reliance on the agency of the state' and the 'heavy state steering and intervention' in the South African higher education transformation agenda and questions what 'sort of transformation will the HEQC project achieve?' In this context, the HEQC (Higher Education Quality Council) is cast as a regulatory agency 'authorised by law to exercise bureaucratic power and (it) is expected to promote the Department of Education's transformation agenda for higher education'. The contrast she creates is between social and individual transformation, and she questions whether this 'transformation project will lead to greater equity and quality in higher education or only to greater equity and political correctness?'

To take stock of the progress made in South Africa on student success is almost the same as taking stock on issues of access and equity. Scott *et al.* (2007) argue:

> It can be argued that the constitution of access and equity as 'issues' in South African contemporary political discourse started with the Freedom Charter and that different sectors of the mass democratic movement had over time various interpretations of the definitions, implications, priorities and strategies necessary to guarantee access to and equity in higher education.

Equity in this context can also be read as redress or transformation. The link with higher education and success was strongly created in policy documents before and after 1994 as Moja and Hayward (2005) demonstrate. Badat (2007) reviews progress made in thirteen years after democracy and paints a very optimistic picture as he argues that 'no domain of higher education has escaped scrutiny and been left untouched, and there have been a wide array of 'transformation-oriented initiatives'. These include:

> the definition of the purposes and goals of higher education; extensive policy research; policy formulation, adoption, and implementation in the areas of governance, funding, academic structure and programmes, and quality assurance; the enactment of new laws and regulations; and major restructuring and reconfiguration of the institutional landscape and of institutions.

He goes on to caution though, that 'the seeds have not been sown in pristine virgin and entirely fertile soil, and the seedlings that have emerged could find their development stifled by long existing, tenacious and deep rooted weeds and choked by pests of various kinds' (Badat 2007). Is structural inequality not part of the 'deep rooted weeds' to choke student success in this country?

De-linking student success from issues of equity, redress and transformation in the South African situation is adopting a limited understanding of the dynamics between ends and means, and between strategies and outcomes. So far tracing the fine thread in this thesis, it is important to note that student success indicators can be defined in terms of (i) participation, (ii) progression (iii) completion and iv) quality of graduates. It would be narrow-minded to reduce 'the quality of the graduates' that Scott *et al.* mention to employability only. A broadened view should include preparing graduates for vibrant careers to enable them to make a meaningful contribution to society as responsible citizens. The challenge in the student success agenda at this stage is to find a means of bringing the purpose of higher education and the debate on graduate attributes closer to each other. This suggests that an embedded indicator has to do with career development – the vision for student success cannot stop at completion, when the students complete their degrees. It should be about the student developing a meaningful career that does not only help in achieving economic empowerment, but one that also makes the individual student to be a responsible citizen who is able to contribute towards positive societal outcomes. It is in this area that the student development programmes developed and implemented by Student affairs can make a meaningful contribution. Needless to say, the efficacy of these programmes will also need to be carefully assessed.

Enhancing student success and understanding learning

The classroom has been hailed as the number one determinant of student success. Good teaching is an important ingredien,t but not the only one in this case. There are promising developments globally and in South African higher education in terms of recognising and rewarding good teaching though the bias towards research has created a big gap that needs serious attention. The failure to give teaching a place of recognition in academia has damaged the desired growth and has stunted innovative approaches from being adopted and expanded on. The teaching and learning award scheme, a joint initiative of HELTASA (Higher Education Teaching and Learning in Southern Africa) and CHE (Council for Higher Education) offers a number of lessons in this regard. Through the scheme we are learning what it means to reward and recognise excellence in teaching when it has suffered neglect over a long period, but more importantly we are learning what it means to go about with a venture like this in an environment where equity and redress remain issues to be grappled with. Refining our thinking on what good teaching is will go a long way in helping us recognise and reward it. The often cited challenge in rewarding good teaching is the argument that there are no well-established criteria to assess good teaching, at least not in the sense that we have come to assess research and research outputs. How far are we from getting these criteria right? Harbouring and incubating bad teaching in our institutions is one strong form of perpetuating structural inequality and the sooner we find ways to improve good teaching and our practices in this regard the better.

Looking at good teaching is a way to investigate the level of agency teachers have in enhancing student success and should not be looked at in isolation. The work of the Physics Professor at Harvard, Eric Mazur is gaining attention as he condemns the lecture method and argues for peer instruction. Quoted on YouTube, Mazur's confession goes like this:

> I thought I was a good teacher until I discovered my students were just memorizing information rather learning to understand the material. Who was to blame? The students? The material? I will explain how I came to the agonizing conclusion that the culprit was neither of these. It was my teaching that caused students to fail!'

He rejects the lecture method as a way of teaching and argues for structured student discussions as a way to engage students in their learning. In my unpublished thesis I have argued that the dominant lecture method is not the only culprit responsible for bad teaching over the years, the much acclaimed Bloom's taxonomy (Bloom 1956) 'has been influential for the last fifty years on what to teach and how to assess learners'. I further argue that some of the effects engrossed into teaching and learning by the taxonomy is the hierarchical and the one dimensional view to knowledge and thinking skills. The limited view to learning, i.e., the transfer of content knowledge from experts to learners, and how to assess the learning thereof, was underwritten by rules coming out of the taxonomy. The revision by Anderson and Krathwohl confirm that the intention of the taxonomy is to 'help educators clarify and communicate what they intended students to learn as a result of instruction' (Anderson & Krathwohl 2001 in Madiba 2009).

In the same thesis I continue to argue that

> What is problematic with the taxonomy is that 'knowledge' was put in the same class as thinking or intellectual skills. The concept 'knowledge' was later replaced by 'remembering' or recall. This added

to the confusion in teaching; content knowledge was conflated with intellectual or cognitive skills and knowing was seen as recall. With these later developments the taxonomy was rewritten into a two dimensional view, to separate the factual, conceptual, procedural and (metacognitive) dimension of knowledge from the cognitive processing (cognitive skill) domain. This revision is highly useful even though the old view is still very persistent. (Madiba 2009)

It is within this context that I differentiate between different learning designs LD (Learning Design) 1/2/3, and the continuum can continue, from the lowest level where content delivery is the main feature, to the next level of learning design, which can be labelled as activity-based learning, and which is a slight improvement on the former but does not provide help to achieve much. The third level, which I label the P/?(B)L learning design, to connote a number of approaches that include problem-based learning, project-oriented learning, case-based learning and inquiry-based learning is a level that provides much hope in terms of what good teaching should look like. A look at the epistemic foundations for P/?(B)L and traditional approaches reveal this contrast from which one can reasonably differentiate between a number of existing 'learning designs' so far as they appear in teaching and learning practice.

Traditional approaches are those where subject specific content is the main (and only essential) feature that receives attention. The goal of teaching and learning is then conceptualised as the transfer of content from expert sources (teachers and books) to the novice learner. The lecture method in its basic form has been one of the main tools in this learning design. I refer to this as LD1. (Madiba 2009)

The use of technology has been hyped and touted as a revolution that will change the face of teaching and contribute to student success. Unfortunately, advancements in technology have not always run side by side with innovations in teaching and learning. In some cases, technology has contributed towards regression rather than improvement in teaching, learning and assessment. The use of quizzes is a case in point. The quality of assessment of learning can become grossly affected if lecturers depend on quick quizzes and poorly designed multiple choice questions for assessment in an attempt to solve the burden of high marking loads. Another point of weakness in the use of technology is the overall faith and confidence placed in learning management systems (LMSs). Many universities adopted the use of LMSs and paid huge license fees, only to realise that the software on its own does not do much. On this issue I quote in my thesis the words of Parkin (2004) who argues that the 'LMS is often the albatross around the neck of progress in technology-enhanced learning.' It became clearer with time that technology-enhanced learning requires substantial technical infrastructure for institutions to see the real benefits. The burden is bigger when participants (users rather) do not recognise the conceptual infrastructure needed to make e-learning tools work for teaching and learning. Conceptual infrastructure is a construct adopted in the thesis to refer 'to the theoretical knowledge and application of models and frameworks necessary to guide the use of technology to enhance teaching and learning' (Madiba 2009). The misappropriation and ineffective use of technology to enhance teaching and learning is another form of perpetuating structural inequality by working against student success and the quality of graduatedness. The current wave of discussions on the 'flipped classroom' offers hope in that the approach seems to creatively move the use of learning technologies away from the traditional lecture method. The innovators of the 'flipped classroom' argue that

> Flipping the classroom has transformed our teaching practice. We no longer stand in front of our students and talk at them for thirty to sixty minutes at a time. This radical change has allowed us to take on a different role with our students. (Bergmann & Sams 2012)

The focus on classroom practice and its link to student success can easily move away from equity and redress issues as good teaching is a challenge to teachers and learners at Harvard as much as it is for any teacher at a historically disadvantaged institution (HDI) in South Africa. A question that arises is whether our explorations of good teaching have been refined to a place where we are able to talk about pedagogies of redress? There is a growing sense in South Africa that in the Extended Curriculum and Foundation Programmes, especially in the foundation part, there are useful pedagogies that are being explored and implemented. One good example is the work reported by Bozalek, Garraway and McKenna (2012) on epistemological access in foundation/extended curriculum programme studies in South Africa. A group of staff members teaching in these programmes was given an 'opportunity to design (or even review) innovative examples of teaching towards epistemological access'. The work was prompted as a result of the recognition that though 'there is widespread agreement amongst practitioners that this is the sort of approach we should be taking there is less overt knowledge about how EA (epistemological access) could be enacted in the classroom.' The compilation is an attempt to showcase ways 'to induct students into the ways of learning'. The concept of epistemological access is an extension of the work instigated by Wally Morrow, which in his view refers to 'learning how to become a successful participant in an academic practice' (Morrow 2000 in Bozalek, Garraway and McKenna (2012). The case studies in the compilation cover interventions such as the 'use of modelling and role-play, peer marking, service learning and language interaction'. There is an acknowledgement that these Extended programmes have made a significant contribution to student success that needs to be amplified in order to experience bigger achievement gains in student success in the sector. The Green Paper attests to this point and reports that there 'has been an increase of 5 per cent in the national student success rate from 69 per cent in 2004 (the introduction of the Foundation Provisioning and Teaching Development grants) to 73 per cent in 2009'.

Closely related to the concept of EA and its value in teaching and learning is the argument made for threshold concepts. A recent press release and call for a conference defines threshold concept in this way:

> A 'threshold concept' can be considered a portal, one that opens up a new and previously inaccessible way of thinking about something. It represents a transformed way of understanding, or interpreting, or viewing something, without which the learner cannot significantly progress. As a consequence of grasping a threshold concept the student may thus have a transformed internal view of subject matter, subject landscape, or even world view.

Exploring the application of EA and the methodological infusion of the treatment of threshold concepts in the curricula taught in higher education are ways of undoing some of the forms of under-preparedness and disadvantage students are faced with. Boughey (2010) indicates that South African AD work experienced a shift in orientation in the late 1980s and 'practitioners took up the challenge to think about 'under-preparedness' in a different way and increasingly began to produce work which was located in (this) critical orientation'. She argues that some of the implications of critical ways of knowing include interrogating the 'idea that success in education is dependent on factors inherent to the individual such as intelligence, motivation and aptitude.' This view resonates closely with the assertion from the Aspen Institute (2004) that 'position and mobility cannot be determined by the subordinated groups'. Boughey (2010) further argues that such interrogation leads to 'how other *structural* factors might be involved in denying success to some groups of students'. Boughey (2010) links an understanding of under-preparedness in students to the 'deficiency model', and further elaborates in this way.

Black students, it is argued, enter higher education with various 'deficiencies' because of the continuing poor performance of the school system (although some people, even in the field of academic development, continue to cite factors inherent to the individual alone, such as 'aptitude'). Locating problems in this way then provides a reason for us *not* to look at the higher education system (and teaching and learning and curriculum practices within that system) to see how and why the system itself could be perpetuating 'structural disadvantage'.

In a research report that was prepared for and commissioned by REAP (Rural Education Access Programme) Jones, Coetzee, Bailey and Wickham (2008) grapple with their own use of the term 'disadvantaged students'. They apologetically indicate that the term is 'used as a shorthand to refer to an array of 'disadvantaging factors' that impact on the ability of poor, rural youth to access and successfully complete higher education studies'. They acknowledge that:

> the use of the term 'disadvantaged students', and indeed other common terminology used, may be misleading insofar as it has the effect of placing the challenges explored in this study at the door of the individual students themselves, and does not give expression to the fact that we believe in the inherent value of human beings and their endeavours.

The 'elephant in the room', to use Wally Morrow's metaphor, is no longer about whether we label these students or not, the new elephant in the room is to identify how far we are perpetuating and entrenching the disadvantage effect, and when are we going to focus more seriously on undoing the damage?

Tinto's (2012) reminder that in order to enhance student success the classroom has to be taken more seriously is set in a context where he argues against 'most innovations (that) have sat at the margins of the classroom and have failed to reach into the classroom to substantially improve the classroom experience'. Tinto takes stock of American higher education reform efforts of the past 20 years and argues that only some and not most of these efforts have made a significant impact. This same accusation was made against Academic Development (AD) over a long period in South Africa (Boughey 2010) and abroad. Stefani (2011) writes and refers to the works of Clegg and Smith (2008) and Clegg (2009) as she acknowledges that 'academic development has moved from being a highly marginal practice to a dominant discourse framing the ways university teaching is understood'. This attests to the fact that over a long period academic development was on the periphery of mainstream teaching and learning and because of such a positioning it could only have a limited impact in the (teaching and learning) improvement agenda, an agenda that is a significant part of improving student success. It has to be acknowledged that there are promising shifts that are occurring where academic development articulates to strategic alignment within universities, with initiatives that are 'viewed as enabling', and academic developers are seen as 'acceptable interpreters and framers working with both senior management and frontline academic staff' (Stefani 2011: 3). These types of shifts offer a lot of hope to the improvement of student success.

Student affairs practitioners can draw lessons from AD practitioners. As already pointed out, for those in academic development the necessary shifts are taking place and these allow academic developers to move away from the periphery and to work closer to the frontline academic staff to improve student success. For student affairs practitioners the challenge is significantly different, it is not about being at the periphery; it is about not sharing the same focus with frontline staff. An analysis of student affairs departments across a number of institutions confirms that the connection to student success is far removed and is seen as indirect. It appears as if the focus on student health, disability, and residences for example reduces these departments to a focus on logistical and operational issues and creates a distance in terms of focus on student success. Appropriating the structural inequality framework within student affairs practice offers possibilities of allowing practitioners in this field to move beyond logistical and operational issues and to find ways to participate in tackling challenges that affect student success.

What is currently happening in the schooling system in South Africa is not helping: the Limpopo textbook saga and the problems the National School Monitoring Survey (*Mail & Guardian* 13 to 18 July 2012) so aptly quantified suggest that we need to stop and pay attention. The saga is a way of assuring us, in the most negative of terms, that for the next number of generations we will continue to talk about the deficiencies Black university entrants bring with them. The results of the survey reported in the Mail & Guardian article validates the research findings in the work edited by Carnoy, Chisholm and Chilisa (2012). Their work is a comparison of South Africa and Botswana entitled *The Low Achievement Trap*, focusing on schooling. They conclude:

> In some sense, the South African policy makers have an easier task, in that South African education production is so inefficient and under resourced in terms of teacher quality that the steps needed to reach Botswana levels of student achievement are more apparent.

And to this 'inefficient and under resourced' teacher quality, one cannot hesitate to add the current textbook saga in Limpopo. Their work paints a clear picture that the educational struggle to be fought today in South Africa is against inefficiency and under resourcing, and to this conundrum we should add the one more vicious fight that should be levelled against the greedy monster of 'tenderpreneurship'. Where are the SASCOs and PASMAs of today? Where is COSAS? Does it mean that these issues do not feature on their radar screen? Why the silence? Perpetrators of today's inequality are those with both the 'sins of commission and omission'.

In another stock-taking work, Fiske and Ladd (2004) conclude their stock taking exercise in this way:

> We conclude that South Africa has made significant progress toward equity in education defined as equal treatment of persons of all races – an achievement for which it deserves great praise. For reasons that we explore, however, the country has been less successful in promoting equity, defined either as equal educational opportunity for students of all races or as educational adequacy. Thus educational equity has, to date, been elusive.

It is this elusiveness that needs focused attention, the kind that will not allow for a glossing over of issues.

What needs to be looked at with caution is the role stereotypes play in this context which is highly infested with structural inequality. The structural racism lens used by the Aspen Institute framework also 'points out that there is national 'common sense' about race – a widely shared set of beliefs and stereotypes – that is revealed in surveys of attitudes about racial groups and in cultural norms.' They warn that 'pervasive assumptions that African-Americans are lazy, violence-prone, and disinterested in family formation' add up to a racialised 'frame'. The recent article, 'Dear Jobless Graduate' by Jonathan Jansen (*The Times*, 21 June 2012), is a typical example of this stereotypical framing. In the article JJ (Jonathan Jansen) continues to frame his JG (Jobless Graduate) stereotype as follows:

> JG is male and female, in the early to mid-20s, mostly black, from a poor family, and from all nine provinces.

And he continues:

> Your marks reveal that you concentrated on passing, and so your 40 per cent in mathematical literacy at school, and your 52 per cent in sociology at university, send all the wrong signals, and here I am not even talking about your meaningless 90 per cent in life orientation.

What JJ misses is that (i) a lot of what he cites as deficiencies he allocates to JG are actually not of his (JG's) own doing, they are structural, and some are built into the curriculum this JG had to take at school, like the much loathed and despised '90 per cent (in) life orientation'; (ii) this stereotype frame has potential to do more harm than help the jobless graduate he is trying to chastise. In this instance JJ greatly misses the point in making a contribution towards undoing structural inequality. Organised student life at South African institutions is one area that needs to be zoomed in the struggle to level the playing field. In the JG stereotype, JJ casts his victim as one who did not take advantage of available opportunities to build an attractive profile that prospective employers would like to pounce on. The characteristics JJ continues to pack on top of this victim question the accessibility of opportunities at the disposal of the JG. How much would student affairs offer to JG in terms of organised student life, especially in the historically advantaged universities, and what is the quality of such programmes? In historically advantaged universities the question might be different: how accessible are these programmes to those individuals from disadvantaged backgrounds? How easy or difficult is it for JG to participate? Since the JG is 'poor', how foreign is the culture of giving; 'giving of one's time' even, as part of 'voluntary work or holiday occupations' and community emgagement?

In their book *Bridges out of Poverty*, Payne, DeVol and Smith (2001) deal with topics such as the additive model: the aha; building an accurate model of poverty; studying poverty research; theories of change and others to make a contribution towards helping communities make sustainable changes and avoid the reactive tactics of dealing with poverty'. We still need this level of research and analysis in South Africa to understand poverty in our context and how to deal with it before we go on with the stereotyping. We need to find ways of working with poor students in our institutions in such ways that do not undermine their human dignity. We should be designing better ways of articulating the hunger we observe in better ways than making these students queue for a meal. Student affairs practitioners have a significant role to play in this regard.

For Tinto (2012) the classroom is central because his frame of reference is American colleges where most of the students he is talking about are those 'who attend two-year colleges, commute to college, work and/or attend part-time'. He points out that for most of these students 'the classroom is one, perhaps the only place, where they meet with academic staff and other students and engage in learning activities'. For South African contact universities, life outside the classroom offers time; many hours that can be channelled into academic work and in a way operationalise the idea of notional hours and academic credits. Learning communities and different ways of organising students into smaller learning groups outside their large classes can go a long way in enhancing student success. The time out of class can also be channelled into those activities that can allow for acquisition of graduate attributes that do not lend themselves easily to development in the formal classroom. One can even push the argument further and argue that organised student life has the potential to provide a platform from which to develop these often touted (graduate) attributes, and allocating university credits that will be part of the graduate profile can be a useful strategy to validate such use of time. The acquisition of university credits outside the formal classroom should not sound as strange, as there are already many benchmarks to work from.

The harshness of the reality in South African higher education is that students from poor backgrounds sit in classrooms where there is bad teaching and, in some cases in institutions that are poorly resourced, to add insult to injury, are taught by teachers who despise putting effort into their teaching strategies and approaches because 'no one will ever recognise that effort'. These students are then trapped in multiple loops of disadvantages where their success is highly threatened. The ripple effect runs wider, to the point where the quality of their graduatedness is made suspect as alluded to in the JJ versus JG referred to earlier in this article. This calls for commitment from all levels of agency to ensure that a reasonable amount of rectification is made.

The REAP report provides hope in that it articulates layers of support that can be put in place to 'rescue' poor students from such traps. The report offers a number of interventions and recommendations that include mentoring, academic advising as well as tracking and monitoring of student support services.

Though Moja and Hayward (2005) argued that individual redress was achieved at a significant scale through funding, especially through NSFAS, the REAP report argues for top-up funds and refined ways of assisting these students for success. The report calls for the private sector to be involved in enhancing student success. The American AtD (Achieving the Dream) movement is an impressive example of how a large cohort of organisations have assembled in the name of student success and degree completion, to an extent that the critics call them the 'completion mafia' (InsideHigherEd 2012). Included in this list is the Bill & Melinda Gates and Lumina Foundation, hailed as two mega-foundations that 'have remade the philanthropic landscape in higher education'.

The AtD movement is an example of 'collective impact' which is contrasted with 'isolated impact' in an article by Kania and Kramer (2011). South Africa has a lot of lessons to learn from this movement. Kania and Kramer (2011) give a useful treatise of what they call 'isolated impact' as they look at 'heroic efforts' and 'failed reforms in the US public education system'. They argue for 'collective impact' instead; 'the commitment of a group of important actors from different sectors to a common agenda'. Through examples they provide, they demonstrate how a group or role-players abandoned 'their individual agendas in favor of a collective approach to improving student achievement' and how these were able to develop shared performance indicators, discuss their progress, learn from each other and align their efforts in support of the common agenda. It is worth noting that, in their statement on the Limpopo textbook saga, the NGO Section 27 (2012) speaks of 'a collective failure of many organisations that represent the poor'.

There are parallels to draw when one looks at the agenda to improve teaching and learning institutionally and nationally. Adopting Kania and Kramer's analysis can be helpful in moving South African role-players with aspirations of enhancing student success away from isolated efforts to work towards what the authors call 'collective success'. Instead of fragmented interventions that target isolated areas improvement, all should rally their efforts and work towards collective impact. Kania and Kramer (2011) suggest five conditions that can 'together produce true alignment and lead to powerful results' and these are (i) a common agenda, (ii) shared measurement systems, (iii) mutually reinforcing activities, (iv) continuous communication, and (v) backbone support organisations. Casting my imaginative net and looking forward, I can envisage how much can be achieved if for example, the HELTASA, SAAIR and SAASSAP communities (to mention a few) could share expertise and strategise together on student success, which should be their common agenda. How much progress can be made in undoing structural inequity if various institutions that claim to have electronic tracking systems could share and build on what is already working rather than working in isolation and spending resources on reinventing the wheel? Another area where this type of talking together is needed is in the area of academic literacy – what forms of provision have proved effective in this area? What data should we look into in order to make data-informed improvement decisions across the sector? The HELTASA Special Interest Groups (SIGs) cannot replace the need to employ a collective strategy. The challenge with the SIGs is that it is HELTASA talking to herself, and would make a big difference to reach out and talk at a broader level and join voices in dealing with the challenges faced by higher education in the country.

The AtD movement as a useful demonstration of how collective impact operates has adopted a set of guiding principles: (i) committed leadership, (ii) use of evidence to improve programmes and services, (iii) broad engagement and (iv) systemic institutional improvement. The movement is devoted toward 'closing achievement gaps and accelerating student success nationwide through efforts on four fronts', namely, (i) guiding evidence-based institutional change; (ii) influencing public policy; (iii) generating knowledge and (iv) engaging the public. The emphasis on leadership is a reminder that poor leadership can add to the multiple traps that disadvantaged masses of students who enter higher education suffer. In other words, poor leadership at all level of educational delivery can perpetuate structural inequity and by so doing greatly undermine efforts in student success.

The principles the AtD movement embraces should be used to inform and strengthen our efforts to enhance student success. The structural racism (structural inequality) framework offers us 'a powerful and promising intellectual tool and it provides valuable insights for individual, organizational, community, and collective action toward (racial) equity'. David Dodson, drawing from the work of the Aspen Institute and in a video presentation at the AtD 2012 conference argues for 'fairness with rigour' and urges that in pursuing such a principle we will end up with 'the quality of being fair'. He argues against the provision of 'equal access without equal opportunity' and convincingly points out that equal opportunity cannot exist when the playing field is not level. The 'fairness with rigour' principle entrenches the data-informed and evidence based approach in the AtD movement and highlights the value of data coaches in the movement. Dodson urges us ask pertinent questions in addressing obstacles that stand in the way of student success, like why barriers exist? And, why structural barriers are hard to remove? Adopting a collective approach and asking these types of questions and rigorously exploring answers will enable us to uncover ways of undoing structural inequality in a systemic manner.

Conclusion

In order to draw the argument in this paper to a conclusion, the picture that emerges in my mind is that of a quilt. How can we quilt together the conceptual, intellectual and practical tools at our disposal to take our efforts on enhancing student success to the next level? The one set of the patches in the quilt are made of the student success indicators: participation, progression, completion and the quality of graduatedness. We need to keep these in front of us, initiating longitudinal studies on specific cohorts and their completion patterns are some of the actions worth engaging in. Another set of patches in the quilt consists of those areas that need refined attention: the classroom, including the rewarding and recognising good teaching; leadership in teaching and learning; and adoption of pedagogies of redress. For student affairs it is not only about the accessibility of quality organised student life, it is about exploring conceptual frameworks that can guide and focus attention on student success in a more direct manner. Other pointers allude to 'sins of commission and omission' like stereotyping the poor students and the noisy silence as the Limpopo textbook crisis unfolds. As far as the quality of schooling is concerned, a relevant effort might be in terms of speaking out at least, and in the process piercing the consciences of those who are directly involved in the perpetration of inefficiency and under-resourcing. In terms of areas where agency needs to be exercised in order to stop partaking in the perpetration of structural inequality, the AtD movement stands as one source of inspiration from which to draw actionable lessons. Mobilising across the nation for collective impact appears to be a move in the right direction.

The image of a quilt suffers a serious limitation as the possibility of falling into some form of reductionism in the struggle of grapple with the many issues that affect student success. Though the patches in the quilt cannot be exhaustive, it remains an attempt to highlight areas that, when attended to, might help in fighting structural inequality as far as it threatens student success.

A return to basics: Selected views on factors preventing access to higher education in South Africa

Lullu Tshiwula and Ncedikaya Magopeni
University of the Western Cape

Summary

The role of higher education and research institutions is to equip a critical mass of skilled and educated graduates, and improving access to higher education is one of the ways in which countries can ensure genuine endogenous and sustainable development. However, it is widely acknowledged that a continuum of factors prevent access to higher education, some of which extend back into early childhood and through all the years of primary and secondary schooling, making their impact felt well before students reach tertiary level. This paper reports on the design and findings of an enquiry that examined some of the realities of access to higher education in South Africa. The study aimed to establish the perceptions of two groups of respondents on what they see as the key factors hindering access to higher education in South Africa. The two groups were: (i) a number of high-school principals from rural parts of the Eastern Cape Province, and (ii) a small group of first and third-year BCom Accounting students who had accessed university study through a foundation programme. The paper delineates the two groups' views and perceptions on the factors that make access to higher education difficult.

Education in South Africa

The system of racial discrimination institutionalised by apartheid in South Africa was particularly evil when it came to the inequities built into the education sector. Its legacy is clearly still a contributory factor to the low throughput rates at both school and university level. However, it is concerning that after almost 20 years of democracy, different and unequal resources (in relation to infrastructure, teacher training, management etc.) within the country's schooling system still prevent the poorest of the poor, that is the majority of the population, from completing their schooling and being able to access higher education.

In our view, South Africa has sufficient resources and enabling policies to make it possible to offer access to higher education to all, as intended in the country's constitution (Act 108 of 1996)[1]. Indeed, since the advent of democracy in 1994, the education sector has cumulatively received the lion's share of state expenditure. Between 1995 and 2009, approximately 7 per cent of the country's gross domestic product and 20 per cent of total state expenditure was allocated to education. However, returns on this investment have been far from ideal. In 2011, while 70.2 per cent of school leavers who wrote the final matriculation exams passed, only 24.3 per cent qualified for university access[2].

The realities of schooling

While the government is working to rectify the imbalances in education, the greatest challenges lie in the poorer, more rural provinces such as the Eastern Cape and KwaZulu-Natal. Schools in the more affluent and urbanised areas of Gauteng and the Western Cape are generally better resourced. Thus, an assessment of government's performance must take into account factors that contribute to the state of education today, as well as the historically relevant limitations.

The national Department of Basic Education is responsible for national schooling policy and oversees schooling across the country as a whole. Each of the nine provinces has its own education department and administrative responsibility lies with them. The governance of schools is further devolved to grassroots level through elected school-governing bodies, which have an important role to play in the running of schools[3]. The key concerns of the poorer-resourced schools can be summed up as follows:

(i) An ongoing lack of infrastructure, including the real basics such as sufficient classrooms, access to electricity, flushing toilets, not to mention school halls, science and computer laboratories or sports facilities.

(ii) Teaching, administrative and governing body skills are less than impressive. For example some teachers are not necessarily qualified to teach the subjects allocated to them and illiteracy levels in some rural governing bodies are high.

(iii) Drop-out rates are high, even in the lower grades where some children are heading households and have to care for their ageing grandparents.
(iv) Learner literacy levels are low, many learners are unable to read English and the fact that English is the medium of instruction from Grade 4 onwards compounds the literacy problem.

The three basic premises of the Finnish schooling system, as outlined by Bloch (2010) offer a useful starting point for raising standards in these schools, namely:
(i) The quality of an education system cannot exceed the quality of its teachers
(ii) The only way to improve outcomes is to improve instruction
(iii) Achieving universally high outcomes is possible only by putting in place mechanisms that ensure that schools deliver high-quality instruction to every child

In terms of effective learning and teaching systems, Finland features among the best education systems in the world. In terms of equity, it aims to create a system that assures every child a quality education irrespective of his or her financial background. Most if not all teachers in Finnish schools have master's degrees in education, and the system, introduced in the early 1970s, sees early childhood as the most important years in a child's education. Sahlberg (2011) contends that the first six or seven years before a child comes to school are the crucial ones, noting that 'if you don't do anything in those important years it is very difficult to catch up. There is no instruction on numeracy and science before a child comes to school, but they have to be exposed to these ideas'.

The state's response

The government is targeting education for the poorest of the poor, with two notable programmes. The first involves increasing the percentage of non-fee-paying schools from 40 per cent in 2012 to 60 per cent by 2014,[4] reducing class sizes in schools serving lower-income communities, and increasing expenditure on school infrastructure. The initiative is carefully directed to the country's most poverty-stricken schools, estimated to comprise up to 40 per cent of all schools in 2007. The programme does not always run as planned, however, and delays or non-payment of subsidies have negatively affected the efficient running of these schools (Bloch 2010: 14).

The second programme is the National Schools Nutrition Programme, which provides a meal for 1.6 million school children every day. In addition, almost 2 000 vegetable gardens have been established in under-resourced schools with the support of the Department of Agriculture, local government structures and a number of non-governmental and community-based organisations (Bloch 2010)[5].

Higher education as a human right

A question that often arises is whether access to higher education is a right, a privilege, or a necessity in South Africa. Part of the answer to this question is contained in the fact that South Africa is a signatory to the 1948 Universal Declaration of Human Rights, and Article 26(1) of that document states, 'Everyone has the right to education' and that 'higher education shall be equally accessible to all on the basis of merit'. Meanwhile, the basic principles of the 1960 UNESCO Convention against Discrimination in Education, which South Africa ratified in 2000, commit the state to making 'higher education equally accessible to all on the basis of individual capacity'.

Furthermore, the World Declaration on Higher Education, adopted by the World Conference on Higher Education in 1998, accentuates the relationship between various levels of education in terms of equity of access; Article 3 of the declaration reads as follows:

> Higher education institutions must be viewed as, and must also work within themselves to be a part of and encourage, a seamless system starting with early childhood and primary education and continuing through life. Higher education institutions must work in active partnership with parents, schools, students, socio-economic groups and communities. Secondary education should not only prepare qualified candidates for access to higher education by developing the capacity to learn on a broad basis but also open the way to active life by providing training on a wide range of jobs. Access to higher education should remain open to those successfully completing secondary school, or its equivalent, or presenting entry qualifications, as far as possible, at any age and without any discrimination.

Essack (2010: 15) also reminds us about plans for a second 'Decade of Education for Africa' as proposed by the African Union and the New Partnership for Africa's Development (NEPAD). Tertiary education features in these plans as one of seven focus areas.

University initiatives aimed at improving access

Admittedly, much work has been put into turning the education sector around. South Africa's higher education system has been extensively restructured since apartheid was abolished in 1994[6]. Badat (2010: 7) notes that, between 1993 and 2008, total student enrolment increased from 473 000 to 799 388. In 1993, 40 per cent of all students were African (191 000 students), and 52 per cent were Black[7].

By 2008, African enrolment had risen to 64.4 per cent (514 370 students) and Black enrolment stood at 75 per cent of total student enrolment.

While these figures point to real improvements, the goal of equal opportunity in terms of access and success is, from a number of critical perspectives, still rather a long way off. For example, South Africa has 11 official languages, of which nine are African languages. And since most of the country's universities were (and effectively still are) single-language institutions before 1994, being able to offer tuition, or even language support, to African students in their mother tongues presents major challenges. Yet not to do so perpetuates a significant inequity.

Virtually all of South Africa's higher education institutions are grappling with the issue of access. The University of Cape Town, which has always been one of the better-resourced tertiary institutions in the country, applies demographic quotas to ensure that more African and coloured students access their institution. This applies particularly strictly to its medical school, which can cater for a limited number of students only. Amidst a barrage of criticism from certain quarters, the university's vice-chancellor, Max Price (quoted in Govender 2010), argues that that the quota system is valid. He notes that:

> using a race-based policy is second best, and it is a proxy for disadvantage most of the time. But our experience shows that a black student coming from a township school who manages 65 to 70 per cent in matric [Grade 12] has overcome incredible odds, we know that if they had been in a good school, they would have got 90 per cent. Therefore we do not want to penalise them because of the accident of the circumstances they were born into. (quoted in Govender 2010)

It is interesting to note that the University of Ibadan in Nigeria has a similar arrangement, whereby a category of students from educationally less-developed states are given special consideration in admission processes even if they have not achieved the requisite marks for the courses of their choice. The programme provides opportunities for at least five such students to be admitted to each department in the institution and is reported to be effective in allowing a greater number of under-represented groups to have access to higher education (EUA 2010).

There are some who argue that preferential treatment aimed at enabling increased numbers of disadvantaged students to access to higher education merely sets these students up for failure. However, a wide range of institutions and state agencies at the Stakeholder Summit on Higher Education Transformation held in April 2010 agreed that access should be widened, and that teaching environments should focus on enabling the success of disadvantaged students in higher education (DHE and CEPD 2010).

Another initiative aimed at increasing access to higher education is the National Student Financial Aid Scheme (NSFAS) which was established by the government in 1999 (see Mdepa & Tshiwula 2011). There are serious concerns that promoting access at the expense of 'quality' scholarship has the potential to change the way universities are viewed and carry out their mandates, but the discord between citizens' declared equal rights to education in South Africa and the real social differentiation in the educational field needs to be explored.

As noted in UNESCO's Declaration on Higher Education for the Twenty-First Century:

> Higher education has given ample proof of its viability over the centuries and of its ability to change and to induce change and progress in society. Owing to the scope and pace of change, society has become increasingly knowledge-based so that higher learning and research now act as essential components of cultural, socio-economic and environmentally sustainable development of individuals, communities and nations. Higher education itself is confronted therefore with formidable challenges and must proceed to the most radical change and renewal it has ever been required to undertake, so that our society, which is currently undergoing a profound crisis of values, can transcend mere economic considerations and incorporate deeper dimensions of morality and spirituality (UNESCO 1998: 2).

Adding further complexity to issues of access, successful throughput, massification and the diversification of students in South Africa, is the fact that globally the sector is undergoing rapid changes. The strong emphasis on knowledge economies, increasing competition among education providers, the increasing number of new providers, developments in technology, the rising importance of internationalisation, and considerable public-funding challenges, are just some of the factors that leaders in higher education have to face.

Henkel (2010: 6, cited in Kubler & Sayers 2010: 31) describes the higher education environment thus: 'Universities have had to equip themselves to confront complexity, novelty and instability, to position themselves in a [...] (collaborative/competitive, public/private) environment that offers high risks as well as opportunities'.

In light of this increasingly complex environment, decision-making and planning for the future remains challenging in the higher education sector. In our view, however, it is important for leaders in the sector to actively *steer* the way into the future, and not just *react* to these quickly changing circumstances. In order for the universities to better respond to the needs of students, it is crucial that they remain in touch with, understand and respond appropriately to the reality of where their most disadvantaged students come from, and the extent to which their most basic needs remain unmet.

The 2009 National Benchmark Tests Project

In addressing the challenges of incoming first-year students, Higher Education South Africa (HESA), a body that represents the vice-chancellors from 23 public universities, instituted a benchmarking project to assess learners' readiness for university study. While not all institutions took part, a mix of formerly advantaged and disadvantaged institutions participated in the study on a voluntary basis.

The study aimed to understand the aptitude of learners already enrolled at universities, and to identify the gaps that require attention. Figure 1 illustrates the national picture in terms of academic literacy levels while Figure 2 shows data from a single formerly disadvantaged institution.

Figure 1: A national picture of academic literacy levels, South Africa, 2009

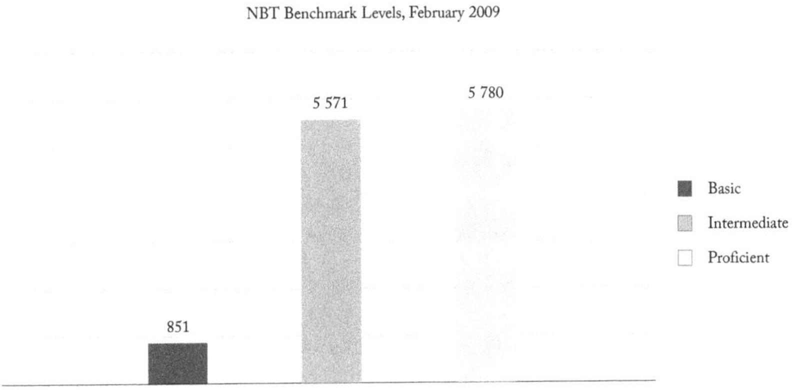

NBT Benchmark Levels, February 2009

- Basic: 851
- Intermediate: 5 571
- Proficient: 5 780

Source: HESA (n.d.: 12).

Figure 1 indicates that a marginal majority was proficient in terms of academic literacy, and a similar number was moderately prepared (intermediate). If one views this on a national basis, it means that to ensure equity of outcomes roughly half of the students enrolled at tertiary level require assistance from university bridging and foundation programmes. Students in the basic category require very extensive support if they are to have any chance of succeeding[8].

Figure 2: Academic literacy levels in the disciplines of commerce, law and science at a formerly disadvantaged institution in South Africa, 2009

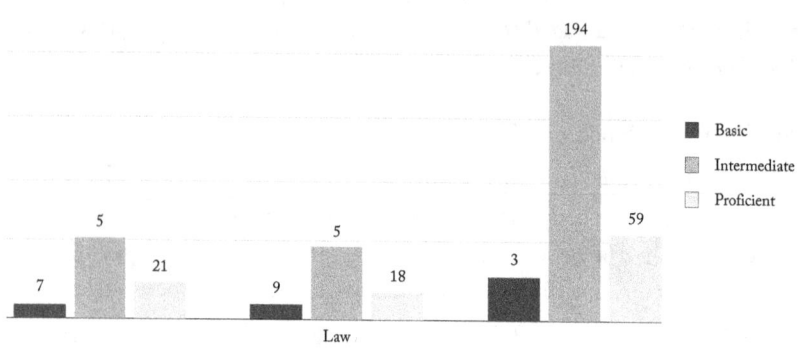

Source: HESA (n.d.: 5).

Figure 2 indicates that far fewer students were considered proficient at this particular campus in the subject areas shown. That is, in all three faculties, the largest single category in terms of academic literacy was the intermediate band. This means that a significant majority of students at the least-resourced institutions require foundation programmes and academic support if they are to succeed at tertiary level.

There is a contention that even foundation programmes are unequal depending on whether students are registered at either a historically disadvantaged or advantaged institution (see Table 1).

Table 1: A comparison of aspects of historically advantaged and disadvantaged institutions, South Africa, 2012

Historically disadvantaged institutions	Historically advantaged institutions
The majority of students are from disadvantaged backgrounds	Compelled by access pressures to accommodate some disadvantaged students
Grappling with how to support learners with inadequate academic preparation	Use strict point systems to ensure selection of the more academically competent students
Funding challenges limit the amount of support that the institution can provide to improve academic success	Some funding challenges but able to draw on financial resources to provide the necessary support to disadvantaged students and help ensure success
The majority of learners receive no instruction via their mother tongue	Many students are taught in their mother tongue, namely, Afrikaans or English

Our study

Having understood the implications of HESA's report on the 2009 national benchmarking tests, we decided to solicit the views of three purposely selected high-school principals from the rural Eastern Cape, and eight Bachelor of Commerce Accounting (BCom Acc) students at a disadvantaged institution who had accessed university through a foundation programme, on the factors that they see as hindering access to higher education in South Africa.

Our aim was to find out about, and understand our research participants' perceptions and experiences of obstacles preventing access to higher education. From school principals we wanted to understand the challenges involved in preparing high-school learners for tertiary study. From the students, we wanted to obtain a perspective on the academic challenges they face at university as compared to their experiences of high school.

Research design
Following research methodologies outlined by Creswell (2007), we decided to use qualitative, descriptive and contextual research methods as we wanted to delve into and understand the meaning individuals and groups ascribe to the particular social problem of access to higher education. The ability to generalise our findings to the whole research population was not part of our goal.

Sampling and data collection
As mentioned, our research participants consisted of two discrete groups. The first group were high-school principals who were purposefully selected for telephonic interviews, namely, they had to be from semi-urban areas in the Eastern Cape. This meant that they were at schools that fall outside the university's usual recruitment area. They had all previously contacted the university to ask for information about how their students could access the university. The second group comprised two first-year and six third-year BCom Acc students (registered in 2012) who had all accessed their degree programmes after completing a university foundation programme. These students were selected for participation in a focus-group discussion. Like the principals, the students were from outside the university's usual catchment area; some came from rural areas in the Eastern Cape and others from rural parts of KwaZulu-Natal.

The students were given a list of topics to reflect on prior to the focus-group sessions. Permission was sought to record both the focus groups and the telephonic interviews and some field notes were taken. Both sets of participants were informed about the study's intentions and signed voluntary consent forms.

They were also informed about their right to withdraw from the study at any time, and the students were assured that no penalties would be attached if they did wish to withdraw. Anonymity and confidentiality were maintained; students were not asked for their names, information gathered was treated confidentially and all audio recordings were destroyed after the analysis had been completed.

Data was collected from the principals via semi-structured telephonic interviews. In other words, we had a set of pre-prepared questions, but the interviews were guided by the schedule rather than dictated by it. Thus the principals were perceived as experts on the subject and were allowed the maximum opportunity to tell their stories.

The focus-group interview was conducted in an informal but respectful atmosphere, and participants were encouraged to share a range of ideas and feelings about their own experiences. As noted by Creswell (2007), focus groups are advantageous when interaction among participants is likely to yield particularly rich information and when time to collect information is limited. Since both of these factors applied in this study, the methodologies chosen seemed well suited to the task at hand.

Creswell (2007: 4) describes qualitative analysis as inductive and as involving an ongoing 'data-analysis spiral'. Essentially, this means that we did not wait for all the data to be collected before starting the analysis. Similarly, De Vos *et al.* (2005) note that analysis of qualitative research tends to be non-linear. Thus, as researchers, we evaluated and interpreted data continually during both the telephonic interviews and the focus group sessions, and adjusted subsequent questions to fill any 'gaps' identified. Our aim was to look for trends and patterns in the data obtained from the two groups of respondents, using transcripts, tapes, notes and memory.

Data analysis

After the telephonic interviews and the focus group discussion, we listened to the recordings independently, and made notes, comparing these with the handwritten notes we had made during the interview processes. We then read the transcripts, searching for common issues and formulating categories and subcategories in line with the themes that had emerged. Of the eight students who took part, there was one who did not participate in the discussion at all.

We also consulted colleagues who are experts in qualitative research methodology as part of a peer-review process,[9] and reviewed some of the existing literature on this issue. It was interesting to note that Young (2009) explored similar questions related to a foundation programme at another University. The focus of that study was on underprepared students who chose to enrol at a historically privileged and advantaged institution. Unsurprisingly its findings show that the challenge of under-preparedness is not peculiar to historically disadvantaged institutions, and presents major challenges to the advantaged institutions as well.

Limitations of the study

We have an overview of co-curricular programmes offered to students in the foundation programme at the university concerned, so there may be a degree of researchers' bias. Our own backgrounds, culture, and history also undoubtedly and unavoidably informed the questions we asked and how we perceived the responses we received.

Findings from the focus group

Students identified major differences in terms of teaching methodology between high school and higher education. This specifically refers to how they had been prepared for their Grade 12 school-leaving examinations. They noted that at school they had been spoon-fed, while on campus they were expected to develop a critical understanding of the work they cover, and to discern the most relevant information for themselves. One participant had this to share with the group: 'When you arrive at university you are surprised as to why students study so early in the year, and you realise after six weeks that your work is overwhelming you'.

Several students mentioned that their high-school teachers had seemed to struggle to fully understand the subject content they were required to teach. Soobrayan (quoted in Snyman 2011: 422) confirms this situation. It was noted that, for many subjects, university classes tend to be huge and students receive very limited individual attention.

Students reported that they would have liked their schoolteachers to have offered more guidance on how to balance the demands of academic study with co-curricular activities. In the words of one participant, 'Teachers should have indicated that university requires consistent work and is less about "having the time of your life"'.

Similar findings are reported by Cross and Mahomed (2010: 88) who state that the experience of university students depends on their perceptions and expectations of the university. These can range from feeling pride at being at the university to desperation caused by alienation. These feelings can be influenced by the inner resources students have, as well as those that they make use of on campus.

Another important theme that emerged from the focus group was that material that students thought they had mastered at school level in accounting seemed almost entirely irrelevant to what they were being taught in university accounting courses. One participant explained this anomaly as follows: 'When you go to an accounting class some of the things are completely new as if you have never done accounting before. My suggestion is to introduce the basic content of what to expect at a university during your Grade 12 studies.'

Almost all the focus-group participants referred to the importance of receiving support from their families at home in addition to support from their institution. Some participants noted that family support was a major part of motivating them to succeed in their studies.

Others noted that poverty and food insecurity was a major part of their experiences of both high school and university. One participant noted that, 'Even though I got support at home I know of many of my classmates who were struggling with both their studies and socio-economically.'

In relation to the foundation programme, all participants in the focus group had found it beneficial. They noted that because their modules were staggered over an extended (four year) period, the foundation programme had allowed them additional time to adjust to the challenges and demands of academic study. The themes and issues that emerged from the focus group are summarised in Table 2.

Findings from interviews with school principals

According to the principals interviewed, poverty plays a key role in limiting access to higher education for example one participant expressed this issue as follows: 'Firstly I can say that some of the challenges relate to economic conditions, unemployment, poverty and the rate of illiteracy in households. Within our community, about 90 per cent of learners stay with their grandparents'. This state of affairs is not uncommon in South Africa, given the prevalence of the HIV/Aids pandemic. A significant number of learners have only their aging grandparents to look after them, while others are burdened with the responsibility of heading their own households, and having to care for younger siblings and sometimes other relatives.

The principals noted that the absence of positive role models affects learners' outlook on life, especially in relation to education. It was felt that if learners could see and experience members of their own community benefiting from further education, they might be encouraged to study further and see themselves as having a wider set of options and career choices. One participant had this to say about the absence of choices confronting students: 'Some of the learners get surprised in January when they get their results and they have passed, then they throw up their

Table 2: A summary of findings from the focus group of first- and third-year students

Themes	Category	Sub-category
The role of educators	Educators at high-school level	• Some teachers struggle with the teaching methodology and subject areas; for example, one participant stated 'teachers would stick to one methodology even when learners did not understand'. • Teachers at school pay little attention to explaining the importance of balancing academic study and co-curricular activities to learners. • Some teachers spoon-feed learners which does not adequately prepare learners for the challenge of increased self-reliance expected at tertiary level. • There is little relationship between subjects taught at high school and at university, and this calls for few adjustments by students e.g. accounting.
Primary and secondary schooling	Educational environment and family support	• Students have to make a massive paradigm shift between school and tertiary study. • Learners lack academic preparedness as well as the support of family and teachers that could help to facilitate their success. • Class sizes at university level tend to be much larger, which limits individual attention. • The absence of career counselling leads to inappropriate choices of high school subjects. • Poverty breeds a lack of hope; high school students need to set goals for their futures or they end up settling for whatever is available in their immediate surroundings. • Students need support from family and significant others. • Students are under pressure to work and contribute to household income after Grade 12. This reduces their chances of advancing into tertiary study.
Higher education	University environment	• Perceptions of university are incorrectly communicated, and students can become complacent about what is expected of them. • Students need to set time aside to study right from the start of the academic year so as to bridge the divide between their experience of high school and the reality of higher education. • Most students found the foundation programme beneficial, because it allowed them additional time to adjust to the challenges of higher education.

arms in despair. They don't know where to go as they did not anticipate passing. I think that, for some of the learners, the problems are economically based, and there is a lack of motivation at home.'

The change in language of instruction from mother tongue to English that takes place in Grade 4 at many South African schools marginalises some learners, particularly those from homes where there is no culture of reading and where access to spoken or written English is minimal. The use of English as the medium of instruction marginalises many learners; those who are not used to speaking English are suddenly expected to be able to read and write in this language. In addition, Snyman (2011: 421) has noted that there has been a 35–36 per cent decline in literacy levels in Grade 3 learners since 2007.

Principals see life orientation classes as a potentially helpful tool, but note that since this subject is not examined, learners don't see it as a critical part of the curriculum and tend not to take it seriously.

The principals reported that teachers often overrule them, especially with regard to performance evaluations. Soobrayan confirms this, and observes that principals tend not to appraise teachers' performance as they should (quoted in Snyman 2011: 422).

The lack of ongoing training and support for teachers was considered another crucial factor by principals. One participant summed this up as follows: 'after two days of training, teachers cannot be expected to fully impart and implement a new curriculum'.

Cohort assessments that have been introduced in schools from about Grade 9 are unable to offer a useful indicator of learners' readiness to progress to the next school level. This means that learners progress to the next class on the basis of their class's performance, as opposed to their individual abilities. However, learners are then expected to write individual examinations in Grade 12 in preparation for university. This system affects learners' understanding of their subjects and denies them a true understanding of their readiness or potential to access and succeed at tertiary level. Table 3 provides a summary of our findings from discussions with the university principals.

Table 3: A summary of findings from telephonic interviews with high school principals

Themes	Category	Sub-category
Socio-economic realities	Unemployment among parents and high levels of poverty	• The general lack of income and other resources means that learners focus on survival, rather than on the long-term benefits of education. • Many learners come from families that are poor and have few role models for learning beyond school. • Some children are looked after by their grannies or are effectively acting as heads of households, sometimes caring for elderly and/or ill relatives. • Goal orientation and planning is lacking among learners. They attend school with no goals, and are surprised if they pass. Hence they scramble access to higher education at the last minute (so-called walk-ins). • Life-orientation lessons could be better utilised to assist learners to cope with schooling and to prepare them for life outside of school including possible options for further education.
Management of the education system	Teacher performance and evaluation	• Performance appraisals tend to be flawed, as the current system relies on peer networks as opposed to objective assessments of real performance. Appraisals and evaluations are linked to annual increments and can be overruled by teacher peers. • The introduction of class visits by the school principal is seen as intimidating, and not welcomed.
Teaching and learning	Teacher qualifications and curriculum	• Learning is in the mother tongue up to Grade 3. The switch to English from Grade 4 is a difficult adjustment for those who have no educational support at home. This is where some learners drop out and although others reach Grade 12, they still struggle with English, and this reduces their chances of success. • Teacher training tends to emphasise methodology leaving some teachers at a loss when it comes to explaining subject content. Teacher training must be comprehensive to ensure holistic teaching and learner support. • Cohort assessment and promotion up to Grade 11 provides no clear indicators of an individual learner's preparedness for Grade 12 and higher education.

Recommendations

The following recommendations derive directly from the students' and principals' views on existing access mechanisms. They suggested that existing development strategies within the education department and universities be strengthened in the following areas:

- Training and support for teachers from both the national and provincial education departments.
- Rural schools should be prioritised for support in relation to infrastructure as well as training for teachers and school governing bodies.
- Universities should work with learners in subject areas that are considered difficult long before they reach Grade 12 to help prepare them for higher education. This could take the form of six-month bridging courses with targeted schools, from which learners have an expressed interest in academic programmes.
- Schools should encourage families to support learners via their school governing bodies and regular parent-teacher meetings.
- Higher education should continue to consider mechanisms to ensure access such as the existing foundation programmes.

Conclusion

This paper set out to examine factors preventing access to higher education. We acknowledge that there is a continuum of educational issues, and that this paper covers only a select few. We believe however, that in the context of massive inequalities outlined, the voices of students and school principals can provide valuable insight into the specific actions and policies geared to widening access to higher education. The picture that emerges from our findings is not new. What is clear however, is the need to continue to focus attention on the existing basic education gaps, using all the available resources more effectively. Failure to address these very basic needs will exacerbate the chronic shortage of scarce skills that is so damaging to South Africa's growing economy.

Notes

1. Article 29 of the South African Bill of Rights (Chapter 2 of the Constitution) reads as follows: 'Everyone has the right to a basic education, including adult basic education; and to further education, which the state, through reasonable measures, must make progressively available and accessible.'
2. 'Matric pass rate improves to 70.2 per cent' *SouthAfrica.info*. 5 January 2012. http://www.southafrica.info/about/education/matric-050112.htm. As noted earlier, however, a high proportion of school learners never reach Grade 12.
3. One cannot help but wonder about capacity building among governing bodies in rural and informal urban areas. In a follow-up study, we aim to explore this question, especially the role of the Department of Basic Education's District Offices in creating the necessary capacity.
4. Non-fee-paying schools receive all their funding from the state and do not charge school fees.
5. See also 'The National School Nutrition Programme', http://www.education.gov.za/TheDBE/DBEStructure/SocialandSchoolEnrichment/NationalSchoolNutritionProgramme/tabid/131/Default.aspx.
6. For example, several higher-education institutions have merged since 2005.
7. Black in this context should be read inclusively, that is, to denote people of African, Indian and so-called coloured descent.
8. At South African universities, the term 'foundation programme' refers to learning activities at the lower end of undergraduate study. The programmes are intended to enable students from disadvantaged educational backgrounds to acquire the academic foundations necessary for succeeding in higher education. Usually of a year's duration, the time spent in a foundation programme does not necessarily guarantee that students will qualify for their choice of further study. If they fail, they may have to relinquish their goals of success in their chosen field. In general, the programmes aim to provide a non-alienating orientation and induction of students into higher education, various forms of support in relation to academic literacy, numeracy and study skills, a correlation between academic and co-curricular programmes, and an early tracking system to alert the academics and co-curricular staff to any early difficulties so that they can take prompt action (Essack 2011).
9. We gratefully acknowledge the assistance of our colleagues, S Terblanche and M de Jager.

The ethical challenges of a student counselling professional: When is discretion permissible?

Hanlé Kirkcaldy
University of Pretoria

Summary

Student affairs practitioners are confronted with clinical practice dilemmas of an ethical nature on a regular basis, such as when clients refuse, resist or reject treatment, especially if these clients are judged to be in dire need of treatment or require referral to other service providers. A client has a right to refuse treatment. However, there is a small group of clients who refuse treatment and in the process causes practice difficulties and ethical dilemmas. The implications of refusal by this particular group of clients within a university setting are explored in this paper. The role of the therapist as a university employee can be in conflict with obligations towards the client. The ethical values of autonomy and beneficence and the obligations towards the university as a third party are pertinent within the context of this discussion. The paper makes suggestions regarding the management of these students.

Introduction

Members of the health science professions are very familiar with the burden of responsibility that is part of their professional lives. It is therefore important to assess the problem and attempt to find a working solution with clients who refuse treatment within a university setting.

This topic highlights what Adshead and Sarkar (2005: 1011a) call the welfare identity and beneficence ideal that is central to the mental health professions. Their paper referred to psychiatrists, but we can safely extrapolate this welfare position and beneficence ideal to include psychologists, social workers, nurses and doctors; in general all health care professionals (HCPs). We identify strongly with the role of caretaker or carer and we are aware of a duty to care for those who put their trust in us.

Yet, this conversely raises the question of whether we should always, under all circumstances be the caretaker or carer. It forces us to momentarily stop and consider: What does this mean? What does such 'keeping' or 'caring' entail? What are the limits of my role regarding clients in my care? This turns the focus on the concept of autonomy, and the movement in recent years towards the client's rights to make independent judgements and decisions about their treatment rather than to accept that the HCP will 'know what is best for me' (Beauchamp & Childress 2001: 176).

When working in a university setting, there is yet another position to consider, namely that of the university as an institution: all of us are employed by the university; all students are registered at the university. Most of our referrals come via the university in one way or another: faculty members, student housing staff, management or fellow HCPs. What about the university's right to ask: What about this student? Or even the university's right to declare: this student should be treated.

Problem statement

It should firstly be acknowledged that not all students who refuse treatment pose management and ethical dilemmas. In South Africa, persons 18 years and older are under general circumstances considered to be legal majors and sufficiently mature children from the age of 12 can give consent for medical treatment to themselves, without the assistance of a parent or guardian (Children's Amendment Act 41 of 2007). As psychological services at student counselling centres are usually free of charge, there generally are no reasons why a student cannot be seen freely and independently. An autonomous person can choose and give consent to therapy. This means that most students are in a position to give or refuse consent, if they are deemed to be autonomous agents.

Furthermore, with most of the clients referred for psychotherapy at student counselling centres, issues of autonomy, beneficence and dual role responsibilities are not necessarily *central* issues in their therapy and management. We should always be aware of these concepts and their implicit presence in our dealings with students. But more often than not, they are not central to the treatment in that they need separate deliberation. Clients are referred, or refer themselves; they are aware of and relatively motivated to address the problems they are facing; they engage freely in the process of therapy and terminate the process when goals are reached. Often, nobody but the client and the therapist are aware that they were there. They may or may not choose to inform significant others of their decision to engage in therapy. There is no third party involvement if they do not wish there to be.

Conversely, there are certain clients that pose greater difficulties in relation to the above-mentioned concepts of autonomy and beneficence. The following instances may be considered in order to guide the discussion and train of thought, but the difficulties are not limited to only these examples:

- Clients who refuse treatment, but experience pressure from the university, student housing or Faculty hierarchy to submit to treatment because of problematic psychological functioning within the hall of residence or faculty system (e.g. suicide attempts, aggressive behaviour and emotional outbursts);
- Clients who refuse treatment, but have limited insight into their psychopathology and are convinced that the problem lies outside themselves (e.g. slowly evolving psychiatric disorders such as delusional disorders, eating disorders, clients not yet actively psychotic but deemed to be in prodromal phases, clients with problematic personality structures, or clients holding certain religious convictions/beliefs that may prohibit treatment);
- Clients registered as students with the Health Professions Council of South Africa (HPCSA) who suffer from possible professional impairment;
- Clients who attempted suicide, but are not interested in assessment or committed to treatment; and
- Referrals from disciplinary hearings

Central ethical issues

According to a dictionary of common philosophical terms, a dilemma is a 'problem where one is confronted with two choices, either of which leads to an unacceptable conclusion' (Pence 2000: 15).

In the above description of treatment refusals, the dilemma is between two core ethical principles in biomedical ethics, namely autonomy and beneficence. These cases pose a clinical, management and ethical challenge. Most therapists would have experienced similar examples and would have formulated their own ideas about how to deal with these challenging cases. The assessment and management plan of therapists would largely have been informed by their basic moral understanding and position. These positions are probably based on the various moral theories such as deontology, utilitarianism, virtue ethics, rights based theories, ethics of care, communitarian or community based ethics and the like. Detailed discussions of moral theories are not within the scope of this paper, but therapists should be aware of their basic moral orientation, as it informs ethical deliberation and substantiates clinical management. The case examples engage the therapist in an interesting ethical discourse as the therapist has to assume an additional role, namely that of a moral agent.

The following basic ethical question may be central to most of these case examples:
- In a university setting, can there be an insistence on therapy, if clients are unwilling and resistant to continue, and if so, under which circumstances?

Less central ethical issues include:
- If student clients refuse or resist treatment, what ethical obligations do we have towards them as clients?
- If student clients refuse or resist treatment, what ethical obligations do we have to the University?
- If these clients were not students, would we consider their management differently?
- What legal obligations are there to consider in certain cases?
- What treatment and management principles should be taken into account?

Relevant central concepts, codes and laws

We have to carefully consider which clients need our special consideration when they refuse treatment. Whatever approach the ethical reasoning about a certain case takes, it is important to keep the following elements in mind: the central ethical concepts, the pertinent ethical codes of conduct for HCPs and the relevant laws of the country.

Autonomy

Ethical codes are based on a 'common morality' that includes four major ethical principles in biomedical ethics: respect for autonomy, beneficence, non-maleficence and justice. Beauchamp and Childress (2001: 58) describe the autonomous person as having the capacities of 'self-governance', such as understanding, reasoning, deliberating, and independent choosing. Those authors declare that the minimum definition of personal autonomy is 'self-rule that is free from both controlling interference by others, and from limitations, such as adequate understanding, that prevent meaningful choice' (2001: 58). Most theories relating to autonomy agree that two conditions are essential for autonomy: liberty, that is (i) the independence from controlling influences and (ii) agency, which is the capacity for intentional actions (2001: 58). This means that a person's right to hold views, make choices and take actions based on personal values and beliefs should be respected and acknowledged (Beauchamp & Childress 2001: 63). Religious beliefs or cultural convictions regarding therapy should therefore be respected. A person's autonomy is diminished, according to these authors, if they are controlled by others in some way or otherwise incapable of acting according to their own choice, desire or plan (2001: 58).

It is important to note that being autonomous and making an autonomous choice is not the same as being respected as an autonomous agent. Beauchamp and Childress reason that autonomous agents can sometimes fail in the act of 'self-governance'. This usually has to do with illness, psychiatric conditions such as depression, ignorance, coercion or other conditions that limit their options (2001: 58). Students who refuse treatment may therefore fail to make autonomous choices due to some of these factors.

The concept of *consent* is another important aspect of autonomy. Eyler and Jeste (2006: 554) state that in order for consent to be valid, it should be fully informed, given voluntarily and by a person with adequate ability to make the decision at hand. Allan (2001) explicates the essential elements of informed consent in terms of the decision maker as follows: he must have adequate information to make the decision, must understand the information on a cognitive level, must appreciate the situation and the consequences of the decision at an emotional level, must have the ability to make a rational decision, which decision must be free and voluntary and s/he must be able to communicate the decision (2001: 31).

Why do we need the consent of the client? According to Beauchamp and Childress, informed consent is a way to minimize the potential for harm, reduce risk, avoid unfairness and exploitation and of course, protect autonomous choice (2001: 77). Some students may be opposed to or do not see the need for treatment, in spite of what the referring agent thinks. They may have been inadequately informed, may not appreciate their situation or fully understand the options open to them, and may change their minds. Certainly however, some may remain convinced that undue pressure and influence have forced them into the therapy room, and that they do not belong there.

Competence is another concept to bear in mind when deliberating about aspects of autonomy. Competence is a complex concept with the basic meaning referring to the ability to perform a task. According to Beauchamp and Childress, standards of competence require certain mental skills (an understanding), certain abilities to comprehend and process information and to reason about the consequences of actions (2001: 72). Allan reminds us that legally competent adults, who have a right to make decisions regarding treatment, also have the right to refuse treatment (2001: 30). He alerts us to the difference between good therapeutic practice on one hand and coercion on the other. Coercion is never acceptable. Adshead and Sarkar mention that there still is the idea that clients diagnosed with any major psychiatric disorder abolish the capacity to make rational decisions. They refer to research demonstrating that patients with mental illness *retain* the capacity to make complex medical decisions, such as treatment options and participation in research (2005: 1012b). In the United States of America, legal decisions have supported the rights of patients with severe mental illness to refuse treatment, even if it had negative outcomes for them (Adshead and Sarkar 2005: 1012b).

The Mental Health Care Act provides for the management of clients who do not consent to treatment, but who are deemed to be in need of treatment. The provisions for such circumstances are described in the act (Mental Health Care Act, 2002 III: 9). In certain circumstances there are legal grounds for intervention. Allan (2008: 104) argues that involuntary detention and compulsory treatment violate people's fundamental rights to liberty and autonomy. He continues to explain that the state justifies these actions on the grounds that it has a duty to protect members of the public as well as a right and a duty to act in the best interest of people who are deemed to be incapable of looking after themselves. Allan alerts us to two additional criteria to those mentioned already, namely that the person must refuse treatment or must be incapable of giving consent to treatment and committal must be the least intrusive way of dealing with the person (2008: 104).

When deliberating on practitioners and students registered with the HPCSA, legal aspects need to be kept in mind. The Health Professions Act makes provision for the HPCSA to investigate and regulate students and practitioners defined by the Act as being impaired. The Act defines impairment as a 'condition which renders a practitioner incapable of practicing as a professional with reasonable skill and safety'. The Act furthermore contains clear directives to report impairment in oneself or in another, (student or practitioner) suspected of impairment or unprofessional, illegal or unethical conduct.

It is useful to differentiate on a conceptual level between impairment, incompetence and unethical behaviour. These are suggested to be related, but not identical, concepts. Describing medical practitioners, Morreim (1993: 19-27) in a Hastings Centre Report proposes the following definitions: The *impaired* physician is defined as unable to practice medicine with reasonable skill and safety, because of physical or mental illness (such as waning eyesight, dementia and substance abuse). The *unethical* physician knowingly and willingly violates fundamental norms of conduct towards others, especially his or her own patients. The *incompetent* physician is not ill but lacks appropriate skills and is ignorant. This seems to be a very useful demarcation of concepts and particularly so because it illuminates to a large extent the strategy needed to manage the healthcare practitioner involved.

While keeping concepts related to autonomy in mind, it becomes apparent that it cannot be the only thing to say about the matter of treatment refusal. What grounds do we have to consider treatment at all, when it is not wanted?

Beneficence

According to Beauchamp and Childress the term beneficence implies that we should act in people's best interests and treat people with welfare (2001: 65). They state that one of the biggest debates in biomedical ethics is whether respect for autonomy should have priority over professional beneficence (2001: 176). Sometimes the therapist may see that there are avenues of action that will be to the client's therapeutic benefit, even though this may clash with aspects of autonomy, such as choice, disclosure of information, confidentiality and privacy.

Adshead and Sarkar identify paternalism as an 'important and sometimes necessary' part of the duty of beneficence (2005: 1011b). They mention that the doctor's duty of beneficence traditionally trumped patients' right to make choices for themselves (2005: 1012a). Because a HCP has superior training, knowledge and insight in certain fields and regarding matters of (mental) health, it may lead to the client being subjected to the position of the ignorant and fearful 'child' (Beauchamp & Childress 2001: 178). Then beneficence can lead to paternalism. The origin of the word suggests the way in which a father will act, presumably towards his children or those in his care. Students are generally young and inexperienced, which makes it so much easier for therapists to be paternalistic in their beneficence. The danger exists that when a student refuses treatment, a HCP may put across courses of action thought to be in the client's best interest, without fully exploring the client's views.

Beauchamp and Childress explain that if a person's known preferences are ignored and action is justified merely by the goal of benefitting or avoiding harm, we are dealing with paternalism (2001: 178). Strong paternalism is when interventions are geared toward benefitting a client who is engaging in risky choices, even though there may be autonomy, voluntariness and information. Weak paternalism protects clients against mostly non-autonomous actions – such as in the cases of severe depression, drug dependency or where there is not enough information and actions in 'the best interest' is necessary (2001: 180).

Beneficence further extends into obligations to assess risks in the case of suicidal and homicidal threats. Paternalism has been the primary justification to intervene in the cases of suicide prevention (Beauchamp and Childress 2001: 188). HCPs may also have duties to warn potential victims if clients make threats against them. Under these circumstances the confidentiality can be broken for the sake of the common good. Gavaghan describes the many difficult aspects of breaking confidentiality in this way, such as the nature of the threat, whether the intended victims are identifiable, a general warning to a group, and the difficulties in accurately predicting the potential for harm (2007: 113-130).

Third parties

Powerful third parties may take a strong paternalistic stance toward clients. A university certainly has legitimate duties toward and claims on student behaviour and conduct. It is, however, my position that universities and agents of a university should not be surrogate parents that can take over decision making for students. Universities do however have rules of conduct to which students and staff must comply. As such, pressure to change behaviour or face disciplinary action and even exclusion from an institution, may be exerted. In the case of an institution however, the utilitarian argument that the behaviour of one student must be weighed against the bigger need and benefit of all, usually prevails. This may be particularly true for students residing on university property. When students are referred on recommendation of a disciplinary board or hearing, treatment refusal is often not an option. The role and function of the HCP will be different than when a student voluntarily seeks treatment.

Other predicaments arise when the student counsellor, as a university employee, must choose between moral duties to the employer and moral duties toward the client. Third parties may attempt to dictate to the therapist and/or the client regarding therapy engagement and process. Clinical judgement and practice may be undermined. Third party pressures can convince therapists that they should proceed in a way that may not be in accordance with what the client truly wishes or not even in the best interests of the client. Callender reminds us that with many clients who present for psychotherapy, the problems originated in the experience of having been used as a means to someone else's ends in the first place (1998: 275). The very process of psychotherapy cannot be seen to reinforce this dynamic. The misuse of therapeutic power and strong paternalistic views are the mainstay of many ethical problems and even complaints against HCPs.

There may therefore be tension between the obligations towards clients and perceived obligations to an institution, a family, or even a society at large. This may result in a conflict of loyalties for the therapist, or the double agent dilemma, also known as double agency or dual roles (Chodoff 1996: 299). Roberson and Walter describe this as 'the dilemma of conflicting expectations or responsibilities, between the therapeutic relationship on the one hand and the interests of third parties on the other' (2008: 229a). They suggest that HCPs (psychiatrists, in their study) adjust to changing times and find an ethically defensible way to manage third party interests, as it is a strong and lasting phenomenon in modern health care (2008 :234).

The strong paternalistic stance of a third party which may very well be based on beneficence must therefore not be confused with the beneficent duty the therapist owes towards a client. Therapists should have the client's best interest at heart, not that of the third party. The relationship between the client and the therapist is different from the relationship between the institution and the student/client. Therapist-client relationships are seen as 'fiduciary', mutual or equitable (Adshead & Sarkar 2005: 1012a), implying that the relationship is based on trust. However, that is not to say that we do not owe duties towards the university as an employer. As Rachels explain, there are however different duties, associated with different virtues (2003: 181). The relationship with a client is different and in a sense more unique than the relationship with an employer. Furthermore, if the trust and fiduciary relationship is perceived to be disregarded by clients, in this case the student population, it is possible that future clients will refrain from seeking help or from divulging important information (Freeman *et al.* 2004: 166). As such, neither the institution, nor the client, or even potential clients, benefit in the long run.

Management suggestions

The appeal for careful balancing of autonomy, beneficence and third party involvement, is grounded in the fear that students with mental illness and emotional problems will somehow become marginalized and treated as different from others. This may lead to a situation where certain students are watched more carefully than others and their actions controlled more specifically, based on psychological criteria. This is a largely discriminatory stance and not defensible.

Keeping the aforementioned theoretical concepts in mind, the following suggestions are made, based on the previous discussions:

Firstly, when clients are suffering from serious mental illnesses, such as psychotic disorders, best practice dictates psychiatric treatment, and possibly admission to a mental hospital. However, until the client presents as an immediate or current emergency, the need for involuntary commitment will in all probably not be necessary. Deliberation of potential risk must be assessed in terms of threat to others, the means in which to achieve it, past behaviour and the like. Therapists working within student health environments would be wise to consult with psychiatry and have well established psychiatric referral systems in place. Involvement of parents usually occurs with the consent of the client. Even after initial refusal, most clients do consent that third parties be contacted after discussion and explanation. If consent is absent and assessment of immediate threat is made, confidentiality could be broken and relevant parties contacted on the grounds of an emergency situation. The challenge for the therapist would be to help the client towards optimal treatment in the least invasive way.

Secondly, clients may be seriously ill, but nevertheless non-psychotic and currently stable. Resistance, denial and refusal of therapeutic engagement are unfortunate, but common phenomena of many diagnostic categories. In many cases it may be a way of coping or attempts at adaptive responses. For therapists, this is 'business as usual'. If attempts to engage such clients in therapy fail, clients should be allowed to exercise autonomous choice and exit therapy. The unfortunate, but unavoidable outcome will probably be that the illness or condition will 'get worse, before it can get better'.

Thirdly, suicidal threats and attempts pose an obvious risk to clients. Duties of beneficence compel us to act responsibly and assess risk and autonomy. In this respect, official and well publicised suicidal policies on university campuses may be helpful (see Meilman & Pattis 1994, for an explanation of such policies). Pillay et al. (2004: 352-360) describe the 'responsible caring' concept in the Canadian Ethical code. This means that the clinician's judgement is not over-determined by autonomous decision making in the client. It allows for routine referral and assessment of clients who displayed non-fatal suicide behaviour. They contend that this does not diminish respect for persons under these circumstances and may comply with a beneficence ideal. Emergency referral options should be available and psychiatric consultant services must be in place and accessible to Student Health Centres, in case of suicide attempts and threats. Many students do not have access to private care and accessing state facilities can be frustrating, slow and dependant on the geographical positioning of the campus. Until such time as these services are optimised, university management may have to come to an agreement with local service providers in their immediate vicinity regarding assistance for students who make suicide attempts and serious threats.

Fourthly, students registered and governed by a professional body, such as the HPCSA, should be made aware of the requirements of the Health Professions Act. Faculties who train these students have an obligation to manage and protect students that may have become impaired. Students must be made aware that they too, ought to manage serious psychiatric (and physical) conditions responsibly, to avoid impairment. If necessary, such students should be registered at the HPCSA Health Committee on completion of their training, for further supervision and management if the impairment persists. Policies that govern and protect HPCSA registered students should therefore be in place at universities.

Fifthly, therapists should not obscure their role to clients and need to take care to explain their function to the client. If clients are referred for an assessment with a report as the expected outcome (as in the case of disciplinary procedures), there cannot be therapeutic expectations and process. Equally important, requests for reports and disclosure of confidential information often occur during therapeutic involvement. Therapists must receive written consent before any information is made available to third parties. It is also important to be able to deny clinical reports to third parties if clients do not consent.

In the sixth place, Jennings *et al.* (2005: 44) state that one of the core values of a good therapist is to be open to complexity and ambiguity, be adaptive and open to find answers and constantly try to overcome obstacles. It seems sensible to acknowledge third parties as important and legitimate role players. Their duties are however not always the same as the duty of the therapist. It may be counterproductive to ignore requests, or take a defensive stance to institutional or parental interests in clients because of one's own anxieties and discomfort. It may be better to manage this pro-actively, in cooperation with the client.

Lastly, it may be helpful to take a preventative, and again not defensive, stance to autonomy and beneficence issues. Therapists may be in a better ethical position if time is routinely taken to discuss issues of autonomy, consent, confidentiality and access to client information, (as well as exceptions to it), therapy contracts, costs and the like, with new clients. Thus consent can be given freely, or not, without due influence and through autonomous choice. This is best done before commencement of the therapeutic process and in a written format to which clients can refer back. Any potential or anticipated problems relating to the referrals can be ironed out by initial discussion. In light of the more problematic cases this process may be imperative. Therapists are in a best position to reframe the referral for a patient. In a sense, cooperation can be negotiated which may be to the benefit of the student as well the institution.

Conclusion

When we return to the problem statement and the ethical questions posed in the beginning of the discussion, we may be in a better position to address the dilemmas we were confronted with. These questions will occasionally come our way when working in a student support environment. Even though the answers are never crystal clear, we should be equipped to negotiate and manage them in a responsible and ethical manner. That is what I intended to achieve through this paper.

Notes

1. A 'profession' has to do with the scope of practice and behaviours associated with a profession, while 'professionalism' refers to the implicit or explicit code of conduct and norms associated with a profession.
2. Bailey (2010) discussed the policy-research nexus and explored the utilisation of research and its impact on policy and in particular the role 'networks' (such as associations) in terms of the interplay between research and policy.
3. The human capabilities approach was originally developed by Amartya Sen (1984, 1995, 2001) and has since been a leading paradigm for policy development around human development issues and was the basis for the United Nations Human Development Index.
4. South African higher education is governed by a policy context which constructs 'Student Development and Support' (the equivalent to student affairs) in a particular way, and any meta-framework needs to comply with national policy. The *National Commission on Higher Education: An overview of a new policy framework for higher education transformation* (DoE 1996: 12) is particularly informative in this regard.
5. *Globalisation* means the global mobility and transnational circulation of information, education, culture, and economics, through the increase in exchange and the opening of borders by the reduction of barriers and the increase of open access to information via the internet and other virtual platforms.
6. The term *neo-liberalism* was coined to describe the period after socio-economic liberalism, which dominated the first world with its emphasis on civil liberty and economic freedom, while protecting individual rights. The removal of the protective regulations sheltering economic monopolies is considered the onset of the neo-liberal economic order.
7. Du Toit (2007) discusses the issues arising from considering, what he called, higher education's 'social contract'. He argued that the social contract safeguards academic freedom and self-determination, a key element for student affairs within the institutions.

The place of social work as a support service for tertiary students

Zethu Mkhize
University of Zululand

Summary

The paper makes the case for the importance of the social work profession in higher education institutions. It highlights the values on which the profession is based, such as the recognition of the worth of each human being and the individual's right to self-determination. It describes the role of the social worker in the context of the triangle of the student, the lecturer and the environment. The paper concludes by discussing the following as the key roles of the social worker: advocacy, facilitator, coordinator, enabler, programme developer and case management.

Introduction

Social workers in an educational setting are an extended arm of the educators in fulfilling educational objectives. According to Skidmore, Thackeray and Farley (1991: 167), social work is one of several disciplines attached to the education system to address and treat problems interfering with the teaching and learning process. Focus of this speciality area has been with reference to a school system and virtually no attention has been paid to the role of social work in institutions of higher learning.

Throughout the world, tertiary institutions are becoming the main social institution for social development. Tertiary institutions are preparing young people to participate in a multinational and global world, bound together by communication and by economic and social relations. According to Friedman (2005: 46) education has become crucial, not only for each person to cope with the demands of modern living, but also for national economic survival. The understanding is that individual young people develop well and that the University supports that development.

Du Toit (2009: 31) contends that the implementation of an outcomes based education system has challenged higher education to develop a specific strategy and well formulated view on how to approach the development of students as individuals. It is for this reason that institutions of higher learning have Student affairs divisions and within them student support units who contribute especially in development areas such as career planning, employability, and self-empowerment. The latter resonates with the mission of social work as a discipline whose object is to develop the full potential of persons, enrich their lives and prevent dysfunction.

Social work is a profession that promotes social change, problem solving in human relationships and the empowerment and liberation of people to enhance well-being. According to the World Summit for Social Development in Copenhagen (2007), social work addresses multiple, complex transactions between people and their environments. Social workers work with young people and their environment, assisting them to accomplish tasks associated with their learning, growth, and development, and thus to come to a fuller realization of their intrinsic dignity, capability, and potential. The basic question that the paper attempts to explore is: What should the role of the social worker be in student support services? Guided by the purposes and needs of education and the learning process, the paper outlines an effective, focused, and comprehensive role of the social worker.

The university community context

The university is conceptualised as a community of students, academic personnel and support staff engaged directly or indirectly in the educational process. Universities are no longer viewed as a building or a collection of lecture halls or theatres where academics and students work together but are also living and learning spaces through their student residences. The university community is not only bounded by geography, comprising all those who engage in the educational process, but is a community where there are varied concrete roles. Each role-player fits into a university community in a particular way to ensure that there is harmony and commonality of purpose. Any obscuring and enmeshment of boundaries tends to have perilous effects on the role performance, thus creating a state of disequilibrium. For instance, management has a responsibility to manage the university while they are thought to be jointly in governance of the university with various stakeholders, including the students through the student governance structures. This is based on the understanding and interpretation of the provisions of the Higher Education Act No. 101 of 1997 but it is likely to create conflict and on-going strife between the university management and the student leadership. This somehow interferes with the core business of the institution and harmony has to be maintained at all cost.

Constable (2008: 121) contends that the education setting is a central place for the development of individuals. It provides a social environment for individuals to grow and develop emotionally and socially. He further postulates that there are often gaps in this relationship, within the education setting and in relation to the needs of the students. He further contends that there are gaps between particular cultures and what the tertiary environment may offer, hence a need for comprehensive student development and support services.

The concept of student development and support services is broadly understood as all those services included in the academic curricular or which directly support and enhance the academic activities of learning and facilitating learning within the higher education institution. These support services include services that have been clustered by Gallagher (1992) as quoted by Du Toit (2009: 20) in his classification system as follows:

- Learning services (e.g. study skills advice)
- Survival services (e.g. counseling)
- Advisory services (e.g. career guidance)
- Recreational services (e.g. fitness)

Student support services seek to develop an exciting, stimulating and supportive campus environment which enhances student learning on multiple levels. It is in relation to this purpose that student development and support functions find their primary purpose within higher education institutions, with the focus being to engage students' potential in order to assist them in achieving their personal and academic goals and to develop responsible and responsive citizens.

The provision of student development services in institutions of higher learning has become an important factor in addressing some of the critical issues in higher education. It is critical that a more holistic approach is applied in the development of the student as a person with specific developmental, supportive and interrelated needs. The complexity of student development as a support function within higher education serves as motivation for defining the role of social work within the student services division. The challenge to the social worker is to help the university community operate as a real community so that personal and community resources can be discovered and mobilised to meet students' developmental needs. The success of the intervention largely depends on the collective and individual involvement.

Rationale for social work services

Social work in education settings is embedded deeply in the roots of society's mandate to the education system to educate and train learners to the maximum of their potential and capacities. Skidmore *et al.* (1991: 177) contend that specialists have been attached to the education system for the purposes of helping individual learners achieve their potential in the academic setting. Social workers focus on social functioning and on the needs of the learners to enable them make the best use of their learning experience.

Social work in an education setting is a specialised area of practice within the broad field of the social work profession. Social workers within an education setting bring unique knowledge and skills to the system and the student support services team. They are instrumental in furthering the purpose of the education institution - to provide a setting for teaching, learning, and for the attainment of competence and confidence. Social workers in student support services thus play a significant role in enhancing the institution's ability to meet its academic mission.

Since its beginnings, social work practice has focused on meeting human needs and developing human potential. Sheafor and Horejsi (2011: 142) state that human rights and social justice serve as the motivation and justification for social work action. In solidarity with those who are disadvantaged, the profession strives to alleviate poverty and to liberate vulnerable and oppressed people in order to promote social inclusion. Social workers practise in the space where individuals encounter one another, where hopes can fail, where gaps exist and where education can break down. Literature has advocated for the recognition of social work in the basic education institutions but as intimated earlier, practically very liitle has been written about social work services in tertiary institutions. The complexity of the tertiary environment and the fact that young persons are entering tertiary at a younger age, suggests that there is niche area for social work. It can make a valuable contribution in assisting students who are marginalised, whether economically, socially, politically or personally. The aim will be to enhance the process of teaching and learning and contributing to student success and development.

Morales and Sheafor (2004: 108) argue that social workers in education settings are expected to apply their professional training in order to support student success. Their capacity to influence student success is clearly influenced by the foundations of social work practice, their skills in assessment and evaluation, cultural diversity, consultative and collaborative relationships and understanding of the role of advocacy and facilitation. Through specialised programmes they can strengthen the students' adjustment at tertiary institutions and address barriers to student learning. Social workers could serve as catalysts in promoting student wellbeing and successful completion of studies.

Social work services at tertiary institutions could be essential to the institutions' ability to accomplish their purpose. The approach to social work practice at tertiary institutions can be predicated on the parameters of the mission of the university, the knowledge and skill of social work, and the social worker's professional responsibility to determine what needs to be done and to develop an appropriate program for doing it. The social worker must be able to determine which needs among the student population can be appropriately met through social work service. The conception would have to focus on the interaction of social work methods and the mission of the university. This would enable the social worker to apply a variety of methods to strike a balance towards achieving diverse student personal goals and facilitating the realization of the complex institutional goals.

Social work is a value based profession and subscribes to a set of cardinal values. One of the cardinal values of the profession is the recognition of the worth and dignity of each human being. Advancing to a democratic society had its own advent in relation to the protection of rights of individuals. This implies that each student should be valued as an individual regardless of any unique characteristic. The reality is that much as the Constitution of the Republic of South Africa Act No. 108 of 1996 makes provision for the protection of the rights of every individual, this is not the case with individuals having certain unique characteristics. This relates specifically to students with disabilities and students with different sexual orientation. If persons with unique characteristics and or attributes can be somehow treated differently by the broader community, universities as centres of excellence and where diversity thrives, would have to lead by example in accommodating these individuals.

The right to self-determination or self-realisation is another value of the profession. Central to this cardinal value of the profession is the respect for individual potential and support for an individual's aspirations to attain such. The right to self-determination affords every person the right to be different from every other and to be accorded respect for those differences. Each student, regardless of race and socioeconomic status, has a right to equal treatment. It is important that individual differences are recognized and intervention is aimed at supporting developmental goals of individual students, hence their significance for social work practice.

Needs of students

The tertiary environment is by its nature liberal due to the absence of community constraints and therefore exposes young persons to multiple temptations which call for constant serious decision making on a daily basis. The HEAIDS sero-prevalence study (2008) has revealed among other things that the newcomer is getting younger. The majority of the students in tertiary institutions are aged between 18 and 25 years. Age is not the only critical factor. With a substantial percentage of the students coming from the disadvantaged communities, this exposes students to the many challenges posed by the tertiary environment, thus interfering with their learning. In the light of the challenges posed by the tertiary environment, there is a need for a proactive strategy to ensure the adjustment of the students. This implies a need for sustained programmes post-orientation. The provision of support towards students' adjustment would best assist in removing barriers to learning, thus enabling the students to make profitable us of their learning experiences.

Most students quickly learn to cope with the everyday challenges of independent living, although from time to time, there may be a need to seek assistance, counseling support or practical advice. It is important to strengthen the existing preventive programmes such that they are effective and behaviour change focused. It is hoped that through mutual exchange of ideas and information, students will be able to make informed decisions about a range of personal problems and or challenges that they face on day-to-day interactions. It is therefore necessary to empower students to take responsibility for their actions. The presumption is that intervention in the lives of the student population must begin early to arrest the course of the problems before they develop into serious challenges.

Students with disabilities

Universities in South Africa have broadened their mission and scope toward becoming more inclusive and toward ensuring the protection of the constitutional rights of young persons with disabilities. This is in line with the provisions of the Constitution of the Republic of South Africa Act No. 108 of 1996 which upholds inclusive education and the objectives of the National Plan for Higher Education which advocates for access and redress. Individuals and young persons who were previously denied and were unable to exercise fully their right to an education have a right to education. It is the responsibility of the tertiary institution to offer persons with disabilities something that would help them to benefit from education. The need for inclusion and differentiated assistance is not just felt by students with disabilities. Lecturers would have to take into account the many different situations and capabilities of their students.

Adjustment to the environment is a real need for students with disabilities. Much as South African legislation prescribes that amenities have to be accommodating to persons with disabilities, the reality of the situation is that this is an ideal that has not been attained by many institutions of higher education. The mobility of students with disabilities is somehow limited and this is likely to impinge negatively on their learning if students do not receive the necessary support. For such support to be meaningful, it is critical that the lecturing staff are fully involved in the process. Institutions through their student support services have to ensure that students with disabilities have positive experiences of tertiary life.

It is worth noting that institutions of higher education have demonstrated their will and commitment in supporting students with disabilities. This is reflected in their active participation in Higher Education Disability Services Association (HEDSA), an advocacy and rights-based organisation representing disability services within the Higher Education Institutions of South Africa. HEDSA's primary objective is to work towards ensuring equal opportunities for all students with disabilities at Higher Education Institutions. Programmes for students with disabilities are in most instances coordinated by officers and or managers with a professional background in social work.

International students

Higher education institutions in South Africa are charting new directions in pursuing their community engagement, scientific research, academic scholarship and publication, teaching and learning in public good in ways that connect with the emerging 'knowledge economy'. In the light of these international trends institutions of higher learning need not only keep abreast of the socio-economic changes in the global environment but also to find an appropriate place for them to flourish in the landscape. Since local regional and global contexts have become increasingly important, it is imperative for the institutions of higher learning to look at themselves as major role players within the Southern African Development Community (SADC) and also as partners in the global village. This means carving a niche for them as to how knowledge would be produced and disseminated. Attracting students from other countries on the African continent requires that support services are provided to address the unique needs of this student population.

It is critical to analyse the intertwining purposes of an academic institution with those of social work. This will best enable an understanding of the role of social work in higher education. Constable (2008: 116) argues that social workers and many educators have come to share similar values. This finds support in the values of the two national councils (i.e. South African Council for Educators and the South African Council for Social Service Professions). These values are predicated on a philosophical belief that each person possesses intrinsic worth and that the needs of people are common. Education institutions are environments where individuals should develop, discover their own dignity and worth, and come to realize their potential. Unfortunately, the human potential of each person is often needlessly wasted. The worlds of young people, often so full of hope, can also be taken over by strange and distorted pictures of human worth and of social relations, hence the significance of enabling young persons to realize their potential.

Social work practice

Social work is a discipline that addresses the barriers, inequities and injustices that exist in society. It responds to crises and emergencies as well as to everyday personal and social problems. Social work utilises a variety of skills, techniques, and activities consistent with its holistic focus on persons and their environments. Its interventions range from primarily person-focused psychosocial processes to involvement in social policy, planning and development. These include counseling, group work, social pedagogical work as well as efforts to help students obtain services and resources in the community. Interventions also include engaging in social and political action to impact social policy and economic development. While the holistic focus of social work is universal, priorities of social work practice will vary from setting to setting depending on cultural, historical, and socio-economic conditions. Tertiary institutions for instance, are working to include those previously excluded from the opportunity of education and the prescribed role of social work is in response to the changing conditions.

The role of the social worker

The basic focus of the social worker is the constellation of the student, the lecturer and the environment. The social worker must be able to relate to and work with all aspects of the student's situation, but the basic skill underlying all of this is assessment which is a systematic way of understanding and communicating what is happening and what is possible. Building on assessment, the social worker develops a plan to assist the total constellation to work together to support the student in successfully completing the developmental steps that lie ahead.

In an ideal situation, the social worker's role is developed by the social worker in conjunction with others, such as the team within the student affairs division. To do this, the social worker needs to have a vision of what is possible, possess tools of analysis, be comfortable with the processes of negotiation, and coordinate the interventions with the life of the university. The roles can be constructed within the context of the university environment. In doing day-to-day work, a social worker is expected to be knowledgeable and skillful in a variety of roles. The role that is selected and used should ideally be the role that is most effective with a particular client, in a particular circumstance and or situation.

In practice, social workers have to perform specific roles in order to ensure that the rights of the students are not violated and that their needs are met. The roles discussed have been adapted from Morales and Sheafor (2004) and contextualized for a tertiary environment. These are the advocacy role, the facilitator role, the programme designer role and the case management role.

Advocacy role: As advocates, social workers act as intermediaries between the students and other systems in order to ensure that the students' rights are protected. Social workers have to use their influence and mandated powers in terms of the Social Service Professions Act 110 of 1978 to be more responsive to the needs of the students. It is then of critical importance for the social workers to establish the availability of a resource in order to have the needs of the students met. Social workers have to identify alternative resources that could be used in order to meet the students' needs.

In performing the advocacy role, social workers have to focus either on protecting the interests of individual students or on the general issues of students' collective concerns. Miley, O'Melia and Du Bois (2001: 337) suggest numerous variables which social workers have to consider in designing advocacy interventions. Among these variables are the availability of resources and the target system's receptiveness of the advocacy effort. The level of intervention is necessary to achieve the desired outcome. Social workers have to consider these variables when performing their advocacy role.

Facilitator role: The basic idea of social work services at tertiary institutions is to assist students to attain a state of well-being. Social workers therefore have a responsibility of continually evaluating the adequacy of services in respect of the needs and problems as presented by the students. Once needs have been assessed, referral to appropriate resource systems have to be made. When exploring the resource network of the students, the social worker has to identify administrative offices within the institution that will be of assistance to the student population. In the event a social worker realizes that some of the offices identified are impinging negatively on the social functioning of the students, he or she performs a facilitative role to ensure that students do benefit from these offices. Social workers, as evaluators, have to evaluate the adequacy of services in respect of the needs and rights of the students, thus facilitating the learning process.

While the Government has responded positively to the educational needs of the students through the provision of NSFAS loans and grants, services should go beyond towards meeting the students' survival needs. Various studies (Masvawure 2008, HEAIDS Sero-prevalence 2008) have revealed that student population is a multiple risk social group, hence there is a wide range of issues that students are wrestling with. The aspect of psychosocial support should also be attended to and social workers have a role to play in the facilitation of psychosocial support for the students.

Guidelines that provide a framework for the identification of vulnerable students have to be developed. Unless action plans are designed, it will always be a challenge for the student support unit to identify students who are in need. Social workers have to collaborate with significant role players in the Student affairs division to facilitate the implementation of the action plans. These include psychologists, coordinators for students with disabilities, coordinators for international students, student governance officers, financial aid officers and bursary administrators.

Coordinator role: Universities are continually confronted with crises situations. This can be as a result of too many things that may be taking place at once or when students are having great difficulty processing a situation. For the institution to manage the crisis at a given time and ensure a safe environment for students, social workers will help develop a crisis management plan for the institution with management and the students. They may coordinate a crisis team, working in different ways with student governance structures and with the broader university population.

Universities have to develop a general plan for dealing with crises, as well as a detailed crisis manual that the social worker, as a key member of the crisis team, helps to create. On hearing about the crisis, the social worker as a coordinator has to make an immediate assessment of the points of vulnerability within the

University and meet with the university crisis team. Using direct counseling and referrals, social workers identify and consider solutions to problems. The main task of the social worker is to focus on making the educational process work to the fullest extent. Their aim is to improve the overall quality of life for the student to be free to learn and to develop and grow.

Enabler role: Social workers in institutions of higher learning may play an important role in gathering information about a student's social, emotional, and behavioral adjustments to the university environment. They may conduct interviews with the student and other significant persons in the student's life, as well as make classroom observations of the student. The latter presumably applies to instances where students might have presented problems related to learning difficulties. Performance of this role applies specifically to students with disabilities and alternative behavioural attributes.

Programme developer role: The social work objective, in its application, is dualistic in the sense that help is not only directed at persons and human groups but also encompasses social conditions that sustain the life of the people in the community. This makes social work a profession of particular importance because it is holistic and takes a total view of human needs. My opinion is that social work practice begins its activity at the point of need as expressed by individuals. Students have specific needs and problems that have to be explored. Social workers may be confronted with the challenge of responding to these needs hence the requirement for the development of a needs-based programme. Social workers may work with a whole institution on developing positive policies and educational programmes dealing with specific needs and or problems identified. When the institution decides to implement a zero-tolerance policy in relation to any untoward behaviour on the part of students, social workers would avail themselves to consult with all the stakeholders on implementation and to work with the students who might be the perpetrators of the behaviour concerned.

Student leadership and governance is one section of student services that is usually fraught with challenges as students sometimes experience tensions and confrontations among one another. In response to such situations, social workers are required to develop violence prevention programs in collaboration with student governance officers. Social workers may develop programmers in response to the issues or problems that are specific to the student population. These may be in response to social issues such as abuse, premature and or unwanted pregnancy, date rape and poverty. They may also include student specific issues related to aggressive anti-social behaviour and or emotional disabilities. They may develop specialized services, provide group counseling on particular topics, and conduct training for peer educators and or peer helpers.

The peer helper programme is a practical example of a programme that is designed to best enable students to mentor new-comers towards adjusting to the tertiary environment. The tertiary environment is liberal in nature and there is no adult who performs constant supervisory role and provide guidance in relation to decision making. Peer helpers provide mentorship thus enabling new comers to adjust and cope with their circumstances. Peer helpers form support groups to assist students to develop coping, social, and decision-making skills. Practice has proved that early intervention is the best strategy to reduce or eliminate stress within or between individuals or groups

Case management role: According to Miley *et al.* (2001: 339) one can trace the impetus for case management to a number of factors which include clients' multiple needs, fragmentation of services, pressure to contain costs in the face of limited resources and funds. The diverse needs of university students befit the performance of this role. The needs of the students have to be met by locating appropriate services among the array of the existing programmes in the student support units. The role of the social worker as a case manager is to ensure that formal and informal resources reinforce each other, thus maximising the benefits of each.

In the view of Austin and McClelland (1996: 1) case management is a pragmatic response to the realities of today's service delivery. They further state that case management links clients to services and aims at meeting a broad range of client-oriented and system-oriented objectives. The social worker, as a case manager in the context of a higher education institution, has to ensure that services given are appropriate to the needs of the students. Social workers have to monitor the appropriateness of services for the students and promote the quality in service delivery. Case management includes not only the assessment of client needs but also the arrangement, coordinating, monitoring, evaluating and advocating for a package of multiple services to meet the specific complex needs of the client. The challenge for case management role in working with the student population is that it may require a big pool of human resources.

Outreach is one of the core functions of case management. The intent of outreach is to heighten the visibility of programmes and services by educating the student population about available programmes. Case finding is a more focused activity of case management that directs outreach efforts toward those who are likely to need the services. Social workers best assist with case finding. It is hoped that through the early identification made possible by outreach, social work intervention with the vulnerable students can prevent problems of a greater magnitude.

Conclusion

Social workers may be involved in a few or all of these roles depending on the nature of their job and the approach to practice that they use. As part of the student affairs team, they may work towards accomplishing the desired goals and strategic objectives of student affairs department. It is of significance that in performing their roles, social workers uphold the dignity and worth of each student in order to build a basis for trust and understanding. Confidentiality is a prime concern with students and all information that is shared with social workers is held in the strictest confidence.

Towards an asset-based model: A critical reflection on student material support with special reference to clienthood/citizenship tension

McGlory Speckman
University of Pretoria and University of Zululand

Summary

The aim of this paper is to reflect critically on the models of student material support in higher education in South Africa. It is argued that current needs-based interventions are one-dimensional, paternalistic and inclined towards a culture of dependency and clienthood as they do not take cognisance of the totality of the disadvantaged student. The less than ideal success rate of NSFAS, the scarcity of resources and the persistent legacy of apartheid provide an opportunity for student affairs practitioners to experiment with models that lead to citizenship. An alternative in the form of an asset-based approach is therefore posited as a way forward[1].

Introduction

The material support for students from disadvantaged[2] backgrounds has always been a challenge in higher education. It is compounded by two factors, namely, the annual escalation in numbers of needy students that enter the system and a lack of satisfactory and effective interventions. Current responses range from amelioration to charitable deeds which neither assist in preventing a further deterioration nor add value to an individual's development. Viewed from a developmental perspective, interventions from both the state and sympathetic individuals within institutions tend to be needs-based and community developers classify this as a deficit model.

It has been argued by community developers such as Kretzmann and McKnight (1993) that communities have never been built upon their deficiencies. Building communities has always depended on 'mobilising the capacity and assets of people and place.' Deficit models are inherently incapable of achieving this for the following reasons: i) resources are never enough to go around and to cover everyone's needs; ii) a deficit model has a 'messianic' approach where the giver or outsider pretends to have all the answers to a community's challenges rather than exploring the solutions a community possesses; and iii) there is always the risk of clienthood whose symptoms have been observed in the last decade and a half of the existence of the National Student Financial Aid Scheme (NSFAS) and other campus charity schemes.

My aim in this paper is to briefly reflect on the current state of affairs with the view to making a case for an alternative approach, the asset-based model. While not denying the realities of the context which necessitates needs-based interventions, I find lamentable what appears to be a replacement of the efforts of students and parents to raise funds for studies during apartheid, by a culture of dependency, non-involvement of parents, minimal productivity and entitlement. Interventions are not meant to be an end in themselves but to enable individuals to develop into responsible citizens. A change in paradigm is necessary in order for this to succeed. If scientific data was easily available, it would be interesting to see how indigenous communities would have dealt with the responsibility of providing for a child's education without hampering its development towards full citizenship. In the absence thereof, it is my view that if conducted within the framework of a holistic vision, the asset-based approach will deliver the desired results for student development.

Following this introduction is a cursory explanation of the terms 'clienthood' and 'citizenship'. The different understandings of 'material support' are discussed in the second section. In the third, words that shed light on our understandings of 'charity', 'beneficence' and 'hand-outs' follow while in the fourth, the context of hand-outs is outlined. A brief discussion and critique of current interventions, perceived as amelioration, follows in the fifth section and is in turn, followed by an outline of the asset-based approach and a conclusion.

Clienthood and citizenship

Clienthood is often juxtaposed with citizenship as if it were a negative concept. The mere focus of this paper on the perceived tension already implies a bias against the concept. However, in social work, clienthood is used in a positive sense, save in instances where the relationship between the client and the social worker becomes corrupted. In the social work theory for example, clienthood is understood as a 'process through which clients become aware of issues, are impelled and sometimes compelled to obtain services, follow various options, come to see an agency as relevant, make contact, are taken into it and processed' (Payne 1997: 1).

A relationship develops between the service provider and the client, formerly referred to as the 'patient' until this was contested as a disempowering term. According to Payne (1997: 3) 'client' has since been preferred to 'patient' since the latter is seen as implying that the person has less autonomy than does the former. Other progressive terms used recently are 'user' and 'customer' which are understood to imply that the individual is more in control than a patient (Payne 1997).

It would seem that the relationship between the client and the service provider becomes corrupt when elements of dependency and lack of initiative creep into the relationship. Mayer and Dufresne list the following in their workshop notes as causes of clienthood: i) substituting programmes for a life; ii) training people to live in the 'disability bubble'; iii) insisting professionals know what a community can and should be and do; iv) equating one or two experiences with failure; v) manufacturing of the need to be dependent on the paid system of supports; vi) reinforcing victimhood self-image; and vii) an entitlement mindset. These look familiar in our context and they are among the risks associated with a deficit model. We may deduce from this that when the relationship reaches this stage in the context of client/social worker, it is possible to talk of a 'social work gone wrong'.

In the social contract theory however, clienthood is seen as a context-specific state. It is not permanent either. Hence Hall *et al.* (2003: 16) advise that clienthood must be separated from the individual. In fact, Payne (1997: 18) goes a little further to assert that clienthood is not 'an absolute state but a process - people are becoming, acting and moving away from being clients of social work.' The route to clienthood begins when someone becomes aware of some issues in their lives which need resolution, 'often this arises from coming to see these issues as a problem' (Payne 1997: 19). To some extent, individuals can have a measure of control although Payne asserts that people's own definition of their status 'does not determine whether they are clients or not' (Payne 1997: 18).

Citizenship on the other hand is understood as in classical times. As Pocock puts it (1988: 32):

> The person is defined and represented through his actions upon things; in the course of time, the term property came to mean first, the defining characteristic of a human or other being; second, the relation which a person had with a thing; and third, the thing defined as the possession of some person.

Pocock is commenting on the Roman idea of citizenship. Romans further associated citizenship with legal protection and the freedom enjoyed under that legal protection as it is clear in the following statement: 'free to act by law, free to ask and expected the law's protection, a citizen of such and such a legal community, of such and such a legal standing in that community' (1988: 32). The term implied rights and responsibilities, particularly the political right to participate in the life of the community, the right to vote and the right to receive certain protection from the community, as well as obligations (Naijamiene n.d.).

In a recent publication, Hamrick, Evans and Schuh (2002: 207) present a different view of citizenship which nevertheless, is appropriate for the context of students. They link it to service learning, leadership development and, I suppose, voluntary activities which are not necessarily based on an individual's academic programme but could, and should be. The elements of responsibility, participation and an ability to take charge of one's destiny seem to be common factors in understandings of citizenship.

At this point, it is appropriate to turn to the prevalent views on 'material support'. It is clear that clienthood has both negative and positive connotations. The former is perhaps the reason for contrasting clienthood and citizenship while the latter is associated with a celebration of rights, freedom, participation and responsibility. This resonates with the student affairs mission of student development. Below I look at material support as an enabler rather than a handout.

Material support as an enabler

There are several views on student material support. The official view may be inferred from the respective founding documents of Tertiary Education Fund of South Africa (1991, 1996) and National Student Financial Aid Scheme (1999) as well as public utterances of politicians. It would seem from these that material support is seen as a means to unlock access to higher education, particularly for students from disadvantaged backgrounds (NSFAS 1999). In other words, material support is driven by equity goals whose aim is to redress the damage caused by the apartheid system. This understanding implies a transcending of financial transactions and a holistic approach to the support of an individual.

Whether the administration of the support (particularly financial support) made available is in tandem with the above goals or not is debatable. Practices at different higher education institutions have varied, particularly at an administrative or distributive level. There seems to be no clear connection in practice between the goal, orientation of beneficiaries from either formal or informal interventions and the administration of assistance. Some students, particularly those from traditionally disadvantaged backgrounds, see the intervention as a right to which they are entitled and there is no demand on the part of the fund administrators for progress-related reciprocation and no intention on the part of the beneficiary to do much more than the minimum requirements in order to remain on the list.

Alongside this official view is the general perception of material assistance, namely charity, which the givers often fail to acknowledge as such. For the purposes of this paper, we have categorized any assistance that is not part of an institutional strategic plan as charity or *ad hoc* intervention. Such schemes are initiated by sympathetic individuals on campus. They are not nutritional programmes as we understand them in other contexts. In its classical sense, charity refers to a relationship between two parties (Speckman 2007: 157). These could be an individual benefactor and the community or the benefactor and an individual beneficiary. As it will become clear in the section that follows below, relationships between individuals were referred to by different Greek terms (eg. *eleemosune* and patron-client) while benefaction/charity (*euergetism*) was broader than that.

Three examples of non-strategy driven and spontaneous campus schemes follow below. The first is the soup kitchen of the University of the Free State. This is tantamount to providing 'daily bread'. Newspaper reports indicate that some 'do-gooders' who include the vice-chancellor's wife provide cooked meals to students on a daily basis. A follow up with the dean of students' office indicated no formal or strategic connection between the sympathetic mothers and the dean of students' office. It was also not clear whether funding for the soup kitchen came from the university budget or not. The only clear connection in the public sphere is that the university has gained public relations mileage out of the project although this was clearly not the aim.

A second example is that of the University of Limpopo at the Mankweng Campus. According to a former dean of students (Masipa 2010), the scheme was started by a group of conscientious staff members who 'could not bear the sight of students whose future was facing erosion by hunger'. The pangs of hunger were so severe that their studies were being impacted negatively. In response, a kitty bag was established by the aforementioned staff members and this led to the birth of a soup kitchen. Five years later, the project was still an *ad hoc* scheme with no financial support from the university. Had anyone offered the hungry students employment or alternatives? There is no evidence to this effect.

In a different context, a third example consists of an initiative by a student structure. Tuks Rag[3] at the University of Pretoria took full responsibility for a scheme that assisted a limited number of needy students with food parcels. In some cases the scheme deposited money into a student's account to enable the student to purchase one meal a day from the campus food outlets which were linked to the university ITS. Beneficiaries were assessed by a Social Worker who also administered the scheme and recommended assistance. The scheme was funded directly by Tuks Rag with funds raised from the public. Most of the students who were assisted by Tuks Rag were referred by the Student Representative Council (SRC). The organization acknowledged that its scheme was not part of the larger Nutritional Programme of the university which was a strategic project of the institution. Hence it assisted any student that was referred to it, whether the student met the criteria set by the university for the institutional feeding scheme or not.

In light of the above, it would seem that material support invariably refers to 'the provision of finance and goods to cover the needs - academic and non - academic, that are deemed necessary for the emotional stability of a student in order to increase their chances of academic success.'[4] I understand it to be an enabler, something that will always be necessary for the success of an aspect of student support. However, it still leaves unanswered questions about whether the intervention is not akin to charity and clienthood as it is needs-based. The following section should shed more light.

Given the concern about the question of student material support as well as its sensitive nature, it is worth balancing the discussion with the hypothetical question: 'What could possibly happen in a situation where there is no material assistance?' Three possible scenarios inferred from the analysis which follows seem to stand out. First, the immediate challenge would be a drop in numbers of students from disadvantaged communities as this was the case before the 'massification' of education in the mid-1990s. Their major hurdle would be the lack of registration fees and minimum payments which would preclude them from institutions of higher learning. As could be learnt from the pre-1995[5] era, campuses with a significant intake of black students faced protests and other actions that disrupted the start of the academic year. Students from historically disadvantaged communities protested against a denial of access based on inability to pay registration fees. This was the case in most institutions. A then President of the South African Students Congress (SASCO), David Maimela (2008/2009), who as a student at the University of Pretoria (UP) had seen the Tsenang Loan Scheme at work at UP, led a SASCO delegation to the Minister of Education, Ms Pandor, to negotiate for NSFAS to cover the registration fees of potential NSFAS beneficiaries. Protests at UP stopped after the Tsenang Loan Scheme was established in 2005 to assist students with academic potential with registration fees and, of course, when the students were included in committees that admitted or excluded students at the faculty level. Maimela wanted to see the former principle duplicated nationally. Although Pandor had agreed in principle, it was only Minister Nzimande who prioritised the need and translated the principle into policy in 2011.

The second scenario would be characterized by a lack of support for the students from disadvantaged backgrounds who managed to gain access into the system. Most of the challenges students face seem to be arising from the apartheid legacy of 'racial capitalism' - in some cases they are confined to individual students while in others they extend to their families. These would include for example, a lack of food for siblings, a lack of accommodation, need for books or lack of money for transport[6]. The emotional support of students speaks to these as they manifest as distractions in various areas of a student's life. Emotional support in this context refers to a support network that is made available to students around any issues that have the potential to lead to emotional upset such as stress, depression, etc. (UP–DSA Plan 2007–2011: 17). Its role is to obviate these by proactively finding ways of addressing them before they aggravate the already stressed emotions.

A third scenario would be a possible acceptance and adjustment to the status quo. This would not necessarily lead to a withdrawal of students from universities but an adjustment to the reality that acceptance into university programmes goes with the responsibility to raise funds for their studies. Academically excelling students ordinarily qualify for merit bursaries save in institutions where some bursaries are still tied to discriminatory clauses and conditions of benefactors who rule from the grave[7]. Parents of students without bursaries have tried their best to finance their children's studies. Most somehow managed without any cattle to sell or having to borrow huge sums of money. There are a number of oral accounts to this effect. This is the ideal scenario in a context where migration from lethargy to independence is prioritised.

I submit that with or without study finance, universities would still have clients and that parents and students themselves would take responsibility for their studies. This has been the case before the establishment of NSFAS when most parents were earning much less than they do today. The official intention with material support seems to be to enable students to gain access and to make success of their studies. In other words, the assistance is intended to be a means to an end. If this aim could be achieved with little or no material interventions, it would indicate that South African Student Affairs is on the path of developing responsible future citizens. Below follows a section that provides a grid to assist in determining whether current interventions facilitate student development or not.

Material support, beneficence and clienthood

The model of intervention (material support) mentioned above, in its various forms, carries a potential to be abused or to lead to dependency and clienthood. A client in this case is a person who is forced by circumstances to be indebted, dependent and subservient to a benefactor who acts as his/her protector. This seems to thrive wherever material support is involved. However, it does not have to be so. A clear outline of the purpose of support given and its goal(s) should help to guard against such unintended consequences. A brief explanation of the respective terms, 'charity' and 'beneficence' and comparison with clienthood will shed more light on the different shades of material support. African Indigenous Knowledge Systems from which we learn that the 'shepherding' of a child to citizenship is a communal effort, is regrettably mostly anecdotal. No documented scientific research could be found for use in this paper although this would have been ideal. Owing to a lack of literary sources, terms from classical times are instead, invoked.

We should at the outset distinguish between the Greek term *eleemosune* which refers to almsgiving, and charity as denoted by the terms 'beneficence' and 'patron-client relations' (Speckman 2007: 157f). The widely held view of charity seems to narrow it down to almsgiving. Yet the latter is confined to subjective responses to situations of need whereas other terms do not necessarily have a subjective element but a business-like transaction based on the principle of 'giving and receiving' (Winter 1994: 46).

The term 'Patron-Client Relations' refers to a relationship between a very wealthy individual and one who is not in his socio-economic rank but is in need of social security (Winter 1994; Garnsey 1988). According to Malina (1988: 211) this relationship was between two unequal persons. Of importance to this paper is the nature of the relationship which was based on mutual obligations. The client bound himself to the patron by undertaking to fulfil certain demands such as the 'morning greeting' and protection in the public arena. On the other hand, the patron undertook to provide food and shelter where necessary as well as legal protection. The client was expected to show gratitude for the gifts bestowed (Winter 1994: 46). Clearly, a contract of mutual benefits was key to the relationship in this case. Unlike in the case of *eleemosune*, reciprocation of favours played a pivotal role and according to Winter (1994) these stood even if there was a recess in the relationship as a result of favourable conditions for the client.

In order for us to appreciate the mutual beneficence aspect better we have to understand that the patron never had a relationship with a person from the bottom classes but with a person from a rank just below him (Speckman 2007: 158). It had to be a person with competencies such as the ability to influence people in certain quarters as well as to rubble-rouse for the patron's gains in the *politeia* (city) (Winter 1994: 48). Malina sums it up well when he says that the two had a 'common bond in the quest for honour' (1988: 21).

The next term in this family of words is '*euergetism*' which is a Greek derivative used to denote beneficence. It refers to beneficence as well as honouring by the community of individuals who 'did good to the city' (Veyne 1990: 10). This was a well- established practice during Greek times and it was continued during the early centuries of the Roman empire (Speckman 2007: 159). The benefactor had an obligation to the society, especially those who voted him into public office, to reciprocate the favour. He was expected to provide food and entertainment, euphemistically referred to as 'bread and circuses' (*Dio Chryssostom* 40: 8). Some provided buildings such as theatres or built aqueducts for water, etc. This was understood to be an obligation even before the prospective benefactor took office.

Veyne (1990: 10) distinguishes between two types of beneficence. The first was the community's expectation that the rich should 'contribute from their wealth to the public expenses, and that this expectation was not disappointed'. In the second place, *euergetism* referred to the benefaction of a voluntary nature which was offered by those elected to public office (ibid.10-11). Of note for the purposes of this paper is that in both cases, the beneficiaries are not individuals; nor were they necessarily the poor. The entire community was the beneficiary (ibid.11). Hence Veyne refers to gifts given as 'collective benefits' (ibid. 12).

The foregoing should suffice to give us an idea of what kind of a contract is preferable for the future generation that must be assisted to create a bridge between an unhealthy past and the hoped for future. There is at least a clear indication of what support is, namely a sharing of 'collective benefits' and what the ingredients of creating clienthood would consist of. These include indebtedness, dependency, non-productivity and possible manipulation[8]. We can only imagine that the risk of becoming dependent on the benefactor results from contours of the relationship not being clearly defined. In classical times, the benefactor gains but there are no obligations on individuals outside the contract. Such contracts existed only between the patron and his client. Benefaction involved the entire community and a distribution of collective benefits. Both the giver and the recipient could make themselves guilty of creating clienthood to the extent that the administration of support could also be used to manipulate. Would this not turn assistance into a hand-out rather than beneficence? Is state intervention not to be seen as beneficence rather than a hand-out which turns potential future leaders into dependents … and beggars? It all depends on how the assistance is administered.

What has come to light thus far is a clear preoccupation with the eagerness to supply or receive. This is known as a needs-based approach or a deficit model (more will be said about it later). While the ultimate aim of this paper is to suggest an alternative to it, an understanding of the context which necessitates giving/supply is crucial.

The context of material support

The context of the issue under discussion is two-fold. On the one hand, there is the immediate context which refers to the manifestations of the problem at the doorstep of the university. This is the primary context to which student support is often directed. On the other, there is a broader context of historical imbalances, manifesting in glaring social inequality as observed in the Green Paper on Post-School Education (DHET 2012), which continue to dog South Africa twenty years into a democracy and of which the manifestations in the immediate context are a by-product. The discussion is divided into four sub-headings.

Bread and butter issues

Higher education institutions are faced with the unenviable task of having to respond to challenges whose origins lie beyond the parameter of the institution, in yesteryear's socio-economic baggage. The problem manifests in various ways at the doorstep of the institution, often with no prospect of a solution. Even what appear to be solutions only amount to *ad hoc* steps which in some cases lead to new problems.

Some manifestations take the form of 'bread and butter' issues. These are summed up in the following excerpt from another context:

> It is no longer shocking when the Dean of Students receives reports about a student or two who regularly spend their nights in the

university's ablutions block or under the shelter of a local train station or at the local filling station. If that is not the case, the Dean of Students' office is inundated with calls from concerned people about students who turn up in class 'looking weak' as a result of hunger or one or two who miss their classes because they are unable to deal with the pangs of hunger. Many students complain about the distance they travel between home and the institution which causes them to only sleep for three to four hours before they board the earliest train or bus or taxi back to campus to attend the following day's classes.

Others request the Dean of Students' intervention in cases where they were unable to present themselves for their semester tests due to inability to find a taxi fare for the day. An occasional cry for assistance with books, photocopy money and accommodation is not foreign to the office of the Dean of Students either (Speckman 2011, Notes for the Senior Management Beraad)[9].

The above list describes the experience of students from disadvantaged backgrounds in a number of institutions, whether affluent or economically struggling. Each of the challenges, no matter how insignificant they might appear to be, distracts a student's attention from the academic business at best, while at worst, they become a stumbling block to an individual's success. In a different context (Speckman 2006) I have alluded to 'pearls hidden in poverty'. This primarily refers to individuals whose development is negatively impacted by unfavourable socio-economic conditions.

Access and retention

Institutions react to material needs because of the widely held perception that mediocre performance and attrition are its direct consequences. The question of access may be positively ascribed to a lack of finances. However, attrition is not as straightforward. Recent limited studies[10] have neither confirmed nor disproved the theory that a lack of finances is solely responsible for attrition although there is a propensity towards questioning it. A study by du Plessis *et al.* (2008) at the University of Pretoria for example, managed to trace 63 per cent of the students who cancelled their studies in 2008. These were drawn from all racial groups and across faculties. Of the four reasons advanced for attrition, those related to material needs only accounted for 7.2 per cent of the total number of students surveyed (Du Plessis *et al.* 2008: 1). A huge percentage (61.9 per cent) advanced career choice or study direction as the major reason for cancelling their studies.

The University of Pretoria had arguably one of the best counseling divisions in the world[11] which had assisted a number of would-be drop outs to stay on course. However, the study has revealed that 69 per cent of the students who cancelled their studies did not make use of the Student Support Division at the University of Pretoria (Du Plessis *et al.* 2008: 2). It would appear that this, more than the lack of material support, could have aggravated the situation.

In a different study conducted on behalf of the Kellogg Foundation (2006-2007), Ludeman has confirmed the negative impact of socio-economic conditions on academic performance (HESA, NASPA presentation 2008). However, the reasons cited in his study range from home language, distance from home, age, finance, etc. Ludeman (April 2013) confirmed by means of an email to me that the 'socio-economic background was cited as *one of the causes* (my emphasis) of attrition'. This corroborates du Plessis' conclusions.

The above findings are corroborated by another independent study (*Focus* March 2013). It is not clear where the study of the Helen Suzman Foundation was conducted and what methodology was utilized. However, its conclusions come close to the conclusion reached by the former two researchers. The study found that there were factors other than economic conditions which determined whether the student stayed on or terminated their studies. These included inter alia, the culture of the institution, a choice of study direction (as hinted at in du Plessis' findings), etc. According to the Foundation's report (*Focus* March 2013), students try to deal with their reality by either finding part-time work or they cancel their studies.

Although in the North American and New Zealand sense attrition is used in the context of discharging oneself permanently from an obligation (*Concise Oxford Dictionary*), for example, a job, the popular view is the military sense. The latter refers to the strategy of wearing out the enemy through acts of attrition, for example systematically bombing strategic positions and key installations before confronting the already demoralised enemy with ground battalions. If it is part of the military strategy to pound the enemy until its energy and capability are worn out, the unfavourable socio-economic conditions as described in the above excerpt, are thought to have had the same effect on the disadvantaged over the years. This might be a reflection of the experiences of some who were confronted with severe socio-economic conditions. Conventional wisdom is that 'all' black students are descendants of the victims of apartheid and that they are still reeling from the 'acts of attrition' resulting from the apartheid policies. I do not necessarily agree.

Mention of the extreme end of attrition is also germane to an analysis of the immediate context of student material support. While normally, attrition refers to a self-discharge from the system before completion of studies, the extreme end of it is that non-performers entrench themselves in the system and stay much longer than they should. The 'trickling in' of support from schemes such as NSFAS seems to result in a 'trickling in' of learning. This dilutes the quality and impacts the value of the degree and access for prospective students.

Learning institutions can never completely ignore the issues of material support although to date, no sustainable or effective solution has been found. Nor is there any overwhelming scientific evidence of a direct link between attrition and economic conditions. Evidence shows that attrition cuts across the economic divide.

Social stagnation

Experience in black communities shows that before the 1990s, it was predominantly children whose parents had the means, who were able to attend university and complete their studies. Yet most students who did not complete their studies in Historically Black Institutions were those expelled for either their political activism or on academic grounds. Very few cancelled their studies due to financial challenges. This situation changed in the mid-1990s, particularly after the creation of a single department of higher education. Students from different backgrounds were suddenly able to study wherever they wished to study, regardless of affordability. However, an intergenerational cycle of poverty constantly placed every new-born child in the category of the indigent with limited economic prospects unless its parents fell in the category of the privileged.

In a different context I alluded to some 'landing on purple cloth at birth while others landed on rags' (Speckman 2009)[12]. Others refer to the former as being 'born with a silver spoon in the mouth'. I went on to argue that the rags they land on tend to follow them throughout their lives even as they attempt to climb the social ladder, as if South Africa subscribes to a caste system. In other words, for a few, there might be upward social mobility while for the majority there is social stagnation. Although opportunities are now being opened up, the historical backlog continually abides with them. Clearly, the solution cannot only be brought about by a focus on material needs. There will never be enough to go around while other vistas could be opened up through a different model of intervention.

Extended family needs

It has become commonplace that the problem begins much earlier and is broader than the demands of the higher education context. For instance, according to recent statistics, of the number of children who register in Grade 1, only 60 per cent of the total number reach Grade 12 (*National School Monitor* May 2012). There are a myriad of reasons for this, including a family background that is characterised by illiteracy. For example, there are two categories of needy students in every institution of higher learning - those who perform academically and are eligible for NSFAS funding and merit bursaries, and others who struggle both academically and financially. The latter are in a 'chicken and egg' situation for they cannot qualify for NSFAS funding until their academic performance improves[13]. Yet their academic performance will not improve unless their socio-economic conditions change for the better.

A number of students in this category find it difficult to cope with having to study while their siblings and other family members are starving. The financial aid given to those who pass the means test is often not enough, while others do not at all have the benefit of financial aid. Curiously, there is little variance in the degree of suffering experienced by the respective two categories. This contradicts the assumption that students with academic potential have a better chance of doing well in their studies since they are primarily supported by the NSFAS (Van der Berg 2013). These students often find themselves in the same situation as the non-funded students, the reason being that their concerns are not only of a financial nature although their use of the funds allocated to them to support their families might be misleading in this regard[14]. Thus, as Tinto found in the American context, their door to higher education is 'only partially open' (Tinto 2008: 1) in that they have no other non-monetary support, therefore, no real opportunity despite access being granted. Hence in some cases, access becomes a revolving door (Tinto 2008). Students gain access but soon find themselves out due to lack of non-monetary but crucial support.

The above context confirms the need. Although it would seem that socio-economic conditions are the source of most of the above challenges, it would be erroneous to regard funding as a quick-fix solution while it is only one aspect of a broader strategy that should be in place to reverse the apartheid legacy. Nor would it be correct to treat the symptom as if it were the actual problem while the problem is much bigger.

Interventions and evaluation

It should be explained at the outset that what is discussed under 'interventions' in this section is in fact, what I earlier labelled as 'amelioration'. Clearly, the situation is grave, aggravated by the global economic challenges at times. However, the quick offer of financial assistance, for example, makes it appear to be better. This resulting in it being seen as improving when in effect, resources are being drained annually with little return on investment. The question is whether the time has not come to experiment with an alternative - whether a paradigm shift is not long overdue?

In evaluating interventions in the above-described situation, the question of the nature of the relationship between the giver and the recipient has to be raised. The original intention, if followed to the letter, is to create better citizens (TEFSA, NSFAS). However, the resources are administered by people who might be seeing a deficit which needs immediate attention, thus opening the intervention up to unintended consequences. Questions therefore have to be raised about whether there are indebtedness, dependency, lack of productivity and manipulation. It also has to be asked what the role of financial aid is in assisting the recipients to reach their full potential or is it merely to get them into the system in order for them to fail? It will not be possible to answer all these questions blow by blow.

On the one hand, there is no scientific proof of a link between attrition and financial constraints. There are only unsubstantiated theories. On the other, it cannot be denied that the students who are affected by the socio-economic conditions are totally inconvenienced by the experience. This makes it difficult to offer an effective solution. As hinted above, in a situation where a needs-based approach is dominant, there always exists a possibility of creating clients out of citizens. A look at the current interventions will shed light on what works and what does not work.

The two common models of support are funding through the National Student Financial Aid Scheme and assistance in kind to which I referred as 'charity' above[15]. An explanation of the latter and different forms it takes is provided. It is however, important to note at the outset, that the former is a political and government treasury response to the problem rather than a Student Affairs intervention. Methodologically, an intervention that is undergirded by the Student Affairs philosophy should always have the twin-pillars of student support and development.

Official documents indicate that the NSFAS is a strategic intervention which is financed by the Treasury, and by extension, the tax payer. It was established in 1999 as a successor to Tertiary Education Fund of South Africa (TEFSA), initially established in 1991. It has as its stated aim the creation of study opportunities for disadvantaged students (NSFAS Act 56 of 1999). However, creating an opportunity is not synonymous with 'carrying' as in taking responsibility for their lives (Speckman 2007: 219-223). It means the creation of capacity for the disadvantaged to study successfully. NSFAS funding assists with tuition, in some cases in full and in others, partially, the latter leading in most cases to perpetual indebtedness.

Universities however, have different ways of implementing the NSFAS vision. Some base the allocation on merit and need, implying that students have to compete for it. Most base it on need alone, meaning that the 50% pass that is prescribed by NSFAS suffices to put the student on the scheme and keep him/her there. Allocations based on merit and need are done on a sliding scale, divided into three categories – 75 per cent upwards, 65 per cent upwards and 50 per cent upwards. Allocations in those categories determine whether subsistence which includes accommodation, study material and basic human needs will be covered. In most cases, those at the bottom only get a portion of their tuition and no subsistence at all.

Universities which adhere strictly to the NSFAS criteria of neediness and 50 per cent pass always have a bigger pool of beneficiaries and insufficient funds to cover all the individual's needs. In order to satisfy all, the existing funds are stretched to reach as many students as possible, resulting in amounts that only cover between 40 per cent and 60 per cent of funding needed by a student for the year. This has present and future consequences. The insufficient amount in a given year results in a student not being able to meet all the needs for his/her success as a student. Yet a continued half-allocation often results in the accumulation of debt even before a student starts working,[16] this running the risk of being written off as a bad debt and the student being blacklisted with the credit bureau, making access to credit virtually impossible. In most cases, the minimum expectation of a 50 per cent pass gives the student enough reason to prioritise everything other than studies as long as they comply with the minimum requirement.

I distinguish between two levels of responses to the problem. The popular response which is almost a default position is to provide for material needs. This is referred to as the 'lower level' response in this paper, my own classification. Proponents of the alternative theory of development would classify [it] as a 'needs-based' response (McKnight 1993, Ammerman & Parks 1998). There is nothing profound or fundamental about it. The needs-based intervention does not advance the search for solutions by a single inch. It does not engage the recipient. No creativity is required from the giver. Hence 'lower level'.

A 'higher level' (which is not where most institutions currently are) entails a response which combines the financial support provided with academic and psycho-social support. The ideal scenario is that recipients are given accommodation, academic support, the material resources they need and their progress is constantly monitored. In this approach, the recipient is fully engaged and the social capital s/he brings is taken cognizance of. It is basically an empowerment model whose benefits may be seen in the performance of Accountancy students who are sponsored by the South African Institute for Chartered Accountants (SAICA) countrywide. In fact, the name of the project, *Thuthuka*, means 'rise up'. Its approach is to create conditions for the bursary holders to realise their potential; in other words, to utilise their assets towards their success. Finance plays a limited role, that of enabling the students to 'relax' and perform. Other aspects of it involve mentorship, academic support and emotional support. This is a requirement of the sponsor, the private sector whose goal is to increase the pool of accountants from historically disadvantaged backgrounds. Regrettably, the model is not duplicated in other areas in supporting students for success despite its self-evident results[17].

It appears that public funding and escalating budgets are set to continue for a long time to come. This is deduced from two things. First, the persistent view that money is a solution to the challenge at hand as stated above. Secondly, even the Ministerial Committee that investigated the impact of the National Student Financial Aid Scheme (2010) fell into the same trap by recommending a further increase of government funding without a proper analysis of the reasons for the 19 per cent (according to their report) throughput rate despite the huge amounts of funds made available annually[18]. It is more the principle behind that recommendation than the statistical data that must be questioned. A 19 per cent success rate after almost two decades of material support should be a good indication that something is amiss rather than a motivation for the allocation of more financial resources.

Government in South Africa in the last few years allocated a few billion rand to NSFAS. According to the Helen Suzman Foundation (*Focus* March 2013), the allocation for 2012 was R5.1bn. In 2013, the allocation has increased. In fact, the Minister of Justice confirmed an amount of R8bn for 2013 during a recent visit at the University of Zululand (August 2013). Yet, if attrition and throughput rates were anything to go by, there would be no justification for the amount. The percentage of throughput rates advanced by the Ministerial Committee on NSFAS (2010) under the chairpersonship of Marcus Balintulo is disputed by Van der Berg *et al.*, in a recent study (summarised in *Focus* March 2013). The latter asserts that previous research had only looked at certain areas and that the Ministerial Committee's Report was only informed by those areas. Van der Berg's study puts the figure of throughput rates at 55 per cent.

Although the full text of Van der Berg's research (a collaboration with others published as Stellenbosch University Working Papers) has thus far not been accessible to me, it is worth responding to at least one aspect of the summary published in the above magazine. Van der Berg's figure derives *inter alia* from the inclusion of the students who have taken much longer than the prescribed period to complete their degrees, calculated over a nine-year period. He ascribes their perseverance to an 'incentive to complete in order to be able to pay back the loan'. This is highly debatable and is contradicted by the debt recovery rate of NSFAS and the throughput rate in some institutions with a number of NSFAS beneficiaries. In his view, the Ministerial Committee did not take this area into account. My response is that it is inconceivable that the time taken to complete a degree or diploma should be regarded as an inconsequential detail in evaluating the impact of NSFAS funding. This reflects a disregard for quality, accreditation and an individual's development. In fact, both figures, that is, the 19% of the Ministerial Committee and the 55% over a lengthy period raise grave concerns about the interpretation and execution of the NSFAS mandate. Is this not a form of paternalism?

It should be clear from the above that the concept of a student financial aid scheme is not being written off completely. In my view, it is the best scheme ever to emerge in the new South Africa. Like most needs-based initiatives, it may be well-intentioned (Eloff & Ebersohn 2001: 150). However, it cannot succeed without the twin programmes of support and development which are essential elements of a holistic approach. In fact, any material support is regarded by the alternative theory of development as providing relief, therefore temporary in nature (Korten 1990). Under scrutiny at this point is the execution of the scheme as a government strategy of addressing the apartheid legacy in the area of education. Has it achieved its goal? Is financial support the only model to pursue? What about the unintended consequences of material support? Is the current approach to NSFAS funding not paternalistic? What is the difference between it and the concepts of *eleemosune, euergetism* and 'patron-client relations'?

Once again, the response to these questions must be reserved for a different study. The Ministerial Committee should have provided the answers. What may be stated without elaborating at this point is that NSFAS (and charity schemes) have had little success. It has not pursued the goal of enabling and has only partially responded to the need for a total redress. The need goes beyond material need and this cannot be addressed through funding alone. This may have opened (in some institutions) the door to a culture of entitlement, paternalism, dependency and a lack of productivity. In short, it may have inadvertently promoted clienthood. The same could be said of campus charity although on a smaller scale.

Although it is still in its pre-implementation stage, the principle of centralizing NSFAS[19] funds and the administration thereof is plausible. It should help in the following ways: i) making it clear that NSFAS is a loan intended to create capacity, not a gift or a right to which anyone is entitled. To this end, conditions which include performance will be strictly adhered to; ii) putting brakes on the development of clienthood which was creeping in as a result of practices in some institutions; iii) demarcating the roles of NSFAS, namely, to provide finance on a business basis; and the institutions, namely, to facilitate the development of the disadvantaged who had been given access, towards becoming full citizens who are independent, self-confident and productive; iv) campus relief schemes will become just that, over a specified period of time and there will be no strings attached. The connotations of 'hand-outs', charity and beneficence which are discussed above and have been associated with NSFAS in some institutions will be eliminated. This should redefine the role of Financial Aid offices and their relationship with the materially needy students.

How does the student affairs practitioner ensure that the above happens in the institutions of higher learning? The removal of NSFAS funds from the institution is no guarantee as there are other needs-based interventions. An effective strategy is one that prevents the development of clienthood while it works towards promoting citizenship. This is the only manner of guaranteeing the holistic support of a student. An asset-based approach is capable of producing the desired results and it is a community development tool. I outline it below albeit in brush strokes. The aim is to introduce the model, not to apply it in this paper. That will need a proper procedure, beginning with a mapping of assets.

Towards an asset-based model

In pursuit of the above, the asset-based approach (A-bA) is presented as an alternative model to be explored in responding to material needs of students in a holistic manner. It is not coincidental that there is a preponderance of black students among the needy but a reflection of the apartheid legacy that must be addressed with a comprehensive strategy. A one-dimensional approach, namely, providing funds as a 'cure' is a copout. It is clear in the Ministerial Report (2010) on NSFAS that it can never be fully effective. By contrast, the situation demands a more holistic approach which looks at material, spiritual and physical needs with an emphasis on assets (tangible and intangible) as the foundation of the initiative. Emphasis should be on the development of the kind of citizen the country needs while funding should only be accorded an enabling role rather than the other way round. A lot could be done with or without funds. The role of the student affairs practitioner in this regard is indispensable.

Both asset-based and needs-based approaches are borne out of responses to human needs. The difference is that one facilitates a process of helping people to help themselves while the other imposes a solution on the people regardless of whether they have theirs or not. But for the asset-based approach, this is immaterial for its focus is on identifying the assets[20] people have to meet their needs and to use that as a moment of empowerment.

What is now widely known as the asset-based approach (A-bA) (Kretzman & McKnight 1993) may also be regarded as a product of the radical theory of development which has since the 1960s critically engaged traditional approaches to development on the dependency they created and the indiscrete pursuits of profits which resulted in the destruction of the environment and caused further underdevelopment (Korten 1990). The radical theory began with an identification of the post-World War II material support as the cause of dependency. It promoted the power of inner resources ahead of material growth (Korten 1990: 67). However, this did not mean a total rejection of well-intentioned relief with a focus on a specific project (Korten 1990).

The A-bA is not necessarily a People Centred Development (PCD) approach in the sense of it focusing on the potential of individuals and communities or targeting social structures or using collective bargaining power to improve people's lives (Korten 1990: 67). However, it is an aspect of the PCD, founded on the principle that solutions to community problems are often located within the community or individuals (Coetzee 1989: 87). A catalyst is needed to unlock these. According to Korten's history of the theory of development, a People Centred Development constitutes the fourth phase, that is, a stage beyond charity, community development and (macro-) policy analysis (1990).

An approach from an asset base affirms the assets, whether material or spiritual, thus forcing the outsider to negotiate any relationship it wishes to have with the community rather than taking it for granted (Eloff & Ebersohn 2001: 149). It cautions against assuming that the community knows nothing, has nothing and is always looking up to outsiders for 'salvation'. The idea is to empower, not to impose on the community. And empowerment is not a one-sided affair. This, incidentally, is a fundamental principle of the ethics of empirical research (cf Hewitt 2007).

The A-bA has been employed by researchers in the last two decades particularly in the disciplines of health (Mokwena 1997), education (Eloff & Ebersohn 2001) and development (Carter & Barrett 2006) with positive results. It offers practical rather than theoretical answers although the initial questions are based on 'spiritual' need thought to be empowerment. In this paper, the same approach is being proposed in a search for an alternative model of student material support owing to the potential it holds for the project. It provides the components that are necessary for a sustainable model. As a bottom-up approach (Eloff and Ebersohn 2001: 150), it places a high premium on the assets of an individual - these being primarily intangible resources, and those of the community which often include physical possessions.

Current and past generations of NSFAS beneficiaries do not seem to appreciate the potential they have within themselves. Those responsible for their development in higher education are partially to blame while the communities they come from are also culpable. The apartheid legacy is used as a limiting, if not crippling, factor while students resign themselves to the fate of victimhood and dependency. Whereas some resort to a culture of entitlement, others become 'clients' of the officials who administer the funds as they are made to believe that they are indebted to them.

The asset-based approach begins not with 'what do you need?' but with 'what do you have that could be of assistance in improving your life further?' Contrasting it with the 'needs-based' or 'deficit-' model, Kretzmann and McKnight (1993) observe that: 'Communities have never been built upon their deficiencies. Building communities has always depended on mobilising the capacity and assets of people and place.' The capacity, skills, knowledge, connections and potential in a community are valued. In this sense, the 'glass is half-full rather than half empty' (*A Glass Half Full*: 7).

By contrast, a 'Needs-based Approach' (N-bA) focuses on the problems, needs and deficiencies (*A Glass Half Full*: 7). It portrays the outsider as the 'saviour' in the situation. Thus much time is spent looking for solutions to problems or fixing problems rather than strengthening the positive or what works in a given community. Eloff and Ebersohn (2001: 149) caution though that the promotion of the A-bA does not necessarily mean that the deficiencies in any given eco-system or sub-system can be negated, but rather that a focus on strengthening the inherent assets in a system, can address the deficiencies'. This is an important distinction.

Eloff and Ebersohn (2001: 149-150) list the following deficiencies of a needs-based approach: i) it runs the risk of being stuck in an endless list of problems and deficiencies; ii) it leads to dependency and disempowerment; iii) it makes resources available solely on the basis of needs thus affecting leadership potential; and iv) it leads to the fragmentation of support as manifested by the levels of cooperation between professionals working through a list of problems and needs. I concur. However, it is not my intention to conduct a discussion of these from scratch as they are already dealt with in Kretzmann & McKnight (1993) and Ammerman and Parks (1998). Suffice it to highlight the fact that points i) to iii) are particularly relevant for the discussion conducted in this paper.

It may be asked whether this is workable in a student context. Students are a community and among them they are endowed with assets that can provide answers to most of their concerns. In addressing the apartheid legacy, practitioners should exploit this. Citizenship implies belonging, that is, to a community. Some of the assets mapped among them for example are: i) social capital; ii) knowledge; iii) intellectual capability; iv) youthfulness; v) technical skills; vi) cash flow; and vii) solidarity groups. There are many more. However, the sample provided should suffice as a point of departure.

Conclusion

The exercise embarked on in this paper has to my knowledge never before been attempted. This is supported by a lack of relevant and value-adding literature on the topic. Some who have alluded to socio-economic factors have done so to support other unrelated arguments such as for example, evaluating government performance on social cohesion since 1994. My perspective was to raise questions about the limited nature of the needs-based approaches and their unintended consequences with the view to making a case for an alternative model.

Pursuant to the above, I have utilised various theories, techniques and approaches in my reflection. These included an examination of the meaning of the terms 'clienthood' and 'citizenship', an outline of classical models of material support, an analysis of the context of material support, a critique of current interventions and an outline of the approach to be explored together with its benefits. It has become clear in the course of the reflection that the dominant model centres around the individual's needs and is therefore a deficit-based approach. It is characterised by negative clienthood as manifested in the escalating dependency, entitlement and minimal productivity. Therefore, it raised the need for a paradigm shift.

In response, I propose experimenting with an alternative that should prepare the beneficiaries for citizenship – whose characteristics are the opposite of clienthood. This cannot be predicated on charity, hand-outs or beneficence but is within each individual and within a community of individuals. However, this does not necessarily mean cashless support but a multi-layered one where the community maps out its capacity, both material and spiritual, to see how it can use those for the education of its young members. An asset-based approach is posited as a model that will draw this out and yield the desired results. The student affairs practitioner should transcend the assumption that they have all the answers 'provided there is funding'. What manifests as material need is invariably symptomatic of a bigger problem which requires a holistic response.

Notes

1. The paper started off as a critique of the attitude of institutions towards needy students on their campuses. I argued that they were insensitive to the plight of the poor and that some of the institutions were creating a revolving door for poor students by accepting them and not providing the material support necessary for their success. A balanced observation later shed light on the mammoth task facing higher education. There are challenges on both sides of the fence. Institutions have to deal with a wider societal problem, the apartheid legacy, while students not only have to contend with the effects of poverty but also with officials that prey on them. Meanwhile, the resources available are not enough to go around and some of those who are likely to secure them tend to adopt a culture of entitlement. With the view to addressing both I changed the focus to an asset-based approach which is not necessarily cashless but has a different departure point.
2. The continued use of the term has been questioned recently by authors such as Kathy Luckett. However, I prefer to use it as is a better understood term by a number of people.
3. A student-run fundraising initiative. It is common in the Western world, having started in Cambridge about 90 years ago. The acronym RAG in the context of the University of Pretoria stands for 'Receive and Give'.
4. This a personally coined definition meant to describe the current state of affairs. Note the emphasis on a student's emotional stability rather than capacity-building, which seems to be the original intention of NSFAS.
5. The start of the year was characterised by protest actions from students who wanted access but did not have registration fees and minimum initial payments. At UP, the situation was finally addressed through the establishment of the Tsenang Loan Scheme by the dean of students to assist those who could not pay at the beginning of the year. Maimela based SASCO's lobbying of the minister on the success of this scheme.
6. These are typical challenges students have to deal with almost on a daily basis and they often expect the deans of students to intervene or assist.
7. Most bursaries from the past have regulations that discriminate in terms of race, language, geographical location and direction of study.
8. Each of these concepts is loaded. However, I will not elaborate on them since the discussion of other terms already paints the picture intended to be sketched in this section.
9. The focus of the presentation at the University of Pretoria Senior Management Bush Summit (Bosberaad) took a different direction precisely because of the fear of institutions to commit their finances to what appears to be a bottomless pit. However, during discussion time, the topic inevitably resurfaced and there was no clear response.
10. I refer to them as limited studies because they were conducted at no more than 8 of the 23 institutions of higher learning in South Africa. Besides, researchers worked mainly with students at historically white institutions. We are not certain whether the outcome would have been the same if the focus had been on historically black institutions.
11. This is no exaggeration. Similar divisions were benchmarked in Singapore, Malaysia, some institutions in the USA, Mozambique and Tanzania.
12. Presentation at the occasion of the acknowledgment of Absa's role in the success of the Mamelodi project which involved Foundation Courses.
13. A 50 per cent pass is all that is expected in order for them to stay on the system. The problem is that 50 per cent of two modules is one module and there is no time frame set for the completion of the study programme.
14. Post-matric studies delay the fulfillment of family hopes for a potential bread-winner who now chooses to be a student instead of trying to find a job – hence the demands on them and feelings of guilt on their part.

15. These are different sides of the same model. They are selected for the purposes of this paper. There are however others such as Eduloan and a myriad of merit bursaries.
16. If a student requires R44 000 to cover the total cost of tuition, accommodation, subsistence, etc., how far is the allocation of R17 000 (around 40 per cent) expected to go and where is the balance expected to come from? That shortfall is likely to occur for three to four years in succession, accumulating more interest along the way.
17. This may sound anecdotal, because there have not as yet been formal academic analyses / reflection on the *Thuthuka* model of support.
18. This figure has been challenged in a working paper published by S. van der Berg *et al.*, of Stellenbosch University (see also *Focus* March 2013). The findings of his team contradict those of the ministerial committee under the leadership of M Balintulo (2010). He puts the figure at 65%.
19. Seven institutions have been chosen for piloting the new model in 2014. Already, there is a lot of dissatisfaction among the students who are potential beneficiaries. This alone is a cause for curiosity.
20. Defined as something that is both acceptable and available, either locally or at another place.

Bibliography

Adshead G and Sarkar SP (2005) Justice and welfare: Two ethical paradigms in forensic psychiatry. *Australian and New Zealand Journal of Psychiatry*, 39: 1011–1017

African Student Affairs Conference (ASAC) (2009, 2010, 2011) Call for papers for African Student Affairs Conference: London: ASAC

Allan A (2001) *The Law for Psychotherapists and Counsellors*, 2nd edn. Somerset West: Inter-Ed

Allan A (2008) *Law and Ethics in Psychology: An International Perspective*. Somerset West: Inter-Ed

American College Personnel Association (1994). *The Student Learning Imperative: Implications for Student Affairs*. Washington DC: ACPA

Ammerman A and Parks C (1998) Preparing students for more effective community interventions: Assets assessments. *Family and Community Health*, 21(1): 32

Anderson L and Krathwohl DE (2001) *A Taxonomy for Learning, Teaching and Assessing: A Revision of Bloom's Taxonomy of Educational Objectives*. New York: Glencoe McGraw-Hill

Aspen Institute (2004) *Structural Racism and Community Building: The Aspen Institute roundtable on community change*. Washington DC: The Aspen Institute. Available at http://www.aspeninstitute.org/

Astin A (1977) *Four Critical Years: Effects of College on Beliefs, Attitudes and Knowledge*. San Francisco: Jossey-Bass

Austin CD and McClelland RW (1996) Introduction: Case Management – Everybody's doing it. *Perspectives on Case Management Practice*. Milwaukee: Families International. pp 1–16

Badat S (2007) Higher education transformation in South Africa post-1994: Towards a critical assessment. Solomon Mahlangu Education Lecture 2007 presented at Centre for Education Policy Development. Constitution Hill, 12 June 2007

Bailey T (2010) *The Research–Policy Nexus: Mapping the Terrain of the Literature*. Cape Town: Centre for Higher Education Transformation (CHET)

Baxter-Magolda M (1992) *Knowing and Reasoning in College: Gender-related Patterns in Students' Intellectual Development*. San Francisco: Jossey-Bass

Beauchamp TL and Childress JS (2001) *Principles of Biomedical Ethics*, 5th edn, Oxford: Oxford University Press

Bergmann J and Sams A (2012) Reflecting on the flipped class from student feedback: online. Available at http://www.thedailyriff.com/articles/how-the-flipped-classroom-is-radically-transforming-learning-536.php [accessed 16 August 2012].

Bernstein B (2000) *Pedagogy, Symbolic Control, and Identity: Theory, Research, Critique*. Lanham: Rowman and Littlefield

Blimling GS, Whitt EJ and Associates (1999) *Good Practice in Student Affairs: Principles to Foster Student Learning*. San Francisco: Jossey-Bass

Botha HL, Brand H, Cilliers C, Davidow A, De Jager A and Smith D (2005) Student counselling and development services in higher education institutions in South Africa. *South African Journal of Higher Education*, 19(1): 73–88

Boughey C (2005) *Lessons learned from academic development movement in South African higher education and their relevance for student support initiatives in the FET college sector:* Commissioned Report. Cape Town: Human Sciences Research Council

Boughey C (2007) Educational development in South Africa: From social reproduction to capitalist expansion? *Higher Education Policy*, 20: 5–18

Boughey C (2010a) *Academic Development for Improved Efficiency in the Higher Education and Training System in South Africa*. Midrand: Development Bank of Southern Africa

Boughey C (2010b) Understanding teaching and learning at foundation level: A 'critical' imperative? In: C Boughey, S McKenna, J Clarence, B Mallison, J Garraway, and J Kioko (eds) *Beyond the University Gates: Provision of Extended Curriculum Programmes in South* Africa. Proceedings of the January 2009 Rhodes University Foundation Seminar hosted by Professor Chrissie Boughey. Grahamstown: Rhodes University Press

Bozalek V, Garraway J and McKenna S (2012) Case studies of epistemological access in foundation / ECP studies in SA: online. Available at http://www0.sun.ac.za/heltasa/mod/resource/view.php?id=50 [accessed 12 July 2012]

Brooks JS and Normore AH (2010) Educational leadership and globalization: literacy for a glocal perspective. *Educational Policy*, 24(1): 52–82

Burke B (1997) International student services: Our business or everyone's business? Keynote address to the Eighth Annual Conference of the International Student Advisers' Network of Australia (ISANA) University of New South Wales, Sydney: online. Available at www.isana.org.au/files/Burke%201997.pdf [accessed 19 December 2009]

Buroway M (2010) Deliberative democracy in a global context: A South African model of higher education? Paper presented at the Stakeholder Summit on Higher Education Transformation, Cape Peninsula University of Technology, Cape Town

Callender JS (1998) Ethics and aims in psychotherapy: A contribution from Kant. *Journal of Medical Ethics*, 24(4): 274–278

Carnoy M (2002) Latin America: The new dependency and education reform. In: H Daun (ed.) *Educational Restructuring in the Context of Globalisation and National Policy*. New York: Routledge Falmer

Carnoy M, Chisholm L and Chilisa B (2012) *The Low Achievement Trap: Comparing Schooling in Botswana and South Africa*. Pretoria: HSRC Press

Carter MR and Barrett CB (2006) The economics of poverty traps and persistent poverty: An asset-based approach. *The Journal of Development Studies*, 42(2): 178–199

Castells M (2001) *Challenges of Globalisation: South African Debates with Manuel Castells*. Cape Town: Maskew Miller Longman

Children's Amendment Act 41 of 2007 (2010): General regulations regarding children, Gazette no. 33076, Notice No. 261, 1 April 2010

Chitnis S (2000) Higher Education in India. *Black issues in Higher Education*, 7: 1-4

Chomsky N (1999) *Profit over People*. New York: Seven Stories

Cilliers CD (2008). Unpublished report. Centre for Student Counselling and Development, Stellenbosch University

Cloete N (2009) Comments on the CHE's The state of higher education report: online. Available at http://www.chet.org.za/webfm_send/558 [accessed 22 December 2009]

Cloete N and Muller J (1998) *South African Higher Education Reform: What Comes after Post-colonialism?* Cape Town: Centre for Higher Education Transformation

Chodoff P 1998 Ethical dimensions of psychotherapy: A personal perspective. *American Journal of Psychotherapy*, 50(3): 298–310

Coetzee JK (1989) *Development is for People*. Johannesburg: Southern Books

Constable R (2008) *The Role of the School Social Worker*. Chicago: Lyceum Books

Constitution of the Republic of South Africa Act No. 108 of 1996

Cosser M and Letseka M (2010) Introduction. In: M Letseka, M Cosser, M Breier & M Visser *Student Retention and Graduate Destination: Higher Education and Labour Market Access and Success*. Cape Town: HSRC Press

Council on Higher Education (2004) *South African Higher Education in the First Decade of Democracy*. Pretoria: CHE

Council on Higher Education (CHE) (2010) *Higher Education Monitor 10*: online. Available at http://www.che.ac.za/heinsa/tl/participants/ [accessed 10 August 2012]

Dalton, J (1999) Racism on campus: Confronting racial bias through peer interventions. *New Directions for Student Services*, 56. San Francisco: Jossey-Bass

Dalton J and Crosby P (2010) How we teach character in college: A retrospective on some recent higher education initiatives that promote moral and civic learning. *Journal of College & Character*, 11(2): 1–10

Dalton JC (1999) Helping students develop coherent values and ethical standards. In: GS Blimling, EJ Whitt & Associates *Good Practice in Student Affairs: Principles to foster student learning*. San Francisco: Jossey-Bass. pp. 45–66

Davidowitz B and Schreiber B (2008) Facilitating adjustment to higher education: Towards enhancing academic functioning in an academic development programme. *South African Journal of Higher Education*, 22(1): 191–206

Dean L (2006) *CAS professional standards for higher education*. Washington DC: Council for the Advancement of Standards in Higher Education

Department of Education (1997) *The Education White Paper 3: A programme for the transformation of higher education*. Pretoria: Government printers

Department of Education (2001) *National Plan for Higher Education*. Pretoria: Government printers

Department of Higher Education and Training (2010) *Report of the Ministerial Committee on the Review of the National Student Financial Aid Scheme*. Pretoria: Government printers

Department of Higher Education and Training (2011) *Green Paper for Post-School Education and Training*. Pretoria: Government printers

De Villiers P, Van Wyk C and Van der Berg S (2013) The first five years project – a cohort study of students awarded NASFAS loans in the first five years 2000–2004. *Working Papers* 11/13. Department of Economics, University of Stellenbosch

Downs C (2005) Is a year-long access course into university helping previously disadvantaged Black students in biology? *South African Journal of Higher Education*, 19(4): 666–683

Downs C (2010) Increasing equity and compensating historically academically disadvantaged students at a tertiary level: Benefits of a Science Foundation Programme as a way of access. *Teaching in Higher Education*, 15(1): 97–107

Du Plessis GI et al. (2007) Exit interviews at the University of Pretoria. Unpublished report, University of Pretoria

Eloff I and Ebersohn L (2001) The implications of an asset-based approach to early interventions *Perspectives in Education*, 19(3): 147–157

Eurostat (2009) The Bologna Process in Higher Education in Europe: online. Available at http://www.ond.vlaanderen.be/ [accessed 15 June 2010]

Du Toit A (2007) Autonomy as a social contract. Council on Higher Education. HEIAFF No. 4. South Africa: online. Available at http://www.che.ac.za/documents/d000143/Autonomy_du_Toit_Feb2007.pdf [accessed 2 March 2012]

Du Toit PH (2009) Providing and Managing Student Development Support in Higher Education In a Developing Country. Unpublished thesis, University of Pretoria

Eyler LT and Jeste V (2006) Enhancing the informed consent process: A conceptual overview. *Behavioural Sciences and the Law*, 24: 553–568

Fang H and Wu W (2006) The professional and academic trends of student affairs in American Universities: In the perspective of evolution of relationship between student affairs and academic affairs. *Comparative Education Review*, 49(1): 83–124

Feldman K, Smart J and Ethington C (2004) What do college students have to lose? Exploring the outcomes of differences in person–environment fits. *Journal of Higher Education*, 75(5): 528–555

Firirey N and Carolissen R (2010) 'I keep myself clean … at least when you see me, you don't know I am poor': Student experiences of poverty in South African higher education. *South African Journal of Higher Education*, 24(6): 987–1002

Fiske EB and Ladd HF (2004) *Elusive Equity: Education Reform in Post-apartheid South Africa*. Pretoria: HSRC Press

Foot J and Hopkins T (2011) A Glass half-full: how an asset approach can improve community health and well-being. Improvement and development agency UK: online. Available at http://www.bankofideas.com.au/Downloads/GlassHalfFull.pdf [accessed 24 February 2014]

Freeman SJ, Engels DW and Altekruse MK (2004) Foundations for ethical standards and codes: The role of moral philosophy and theory in Ethics. *Counseling and Values*, 48: 163–173

Friedman T (2005) *A Brief History of the Twenty-First Century: The world is flat*. Minnesota: New Times

Garci'a-Aracil A (2009) European graduates' level of satisfaction with higher education. *Higher Education*, 57(1): 1–21

Garnsey P (1970) *Social Status and Legal Privilege in the Roman Empire*. Oxford: Clarendon

Garraway J (2010) Field knowledge and learning on foundation programmes. In: C Hutchings & J Garraway (eds) *Beyond the University Gates: Provision of Extended Curriculum Programmes in South Africa*. Grahamstown: Rhodes University Press

Gavaghan C 2007 Dangerous patients and duties to warn: a European Human Rights perspective. *European Journal of Health Law*, 14: 113–130

George K and Raman R (2009) Case study: Changes in Indian higher education – An insider's view. Unpublished paper as support material for *Transformation in Higher Education*. Cape Town: Centre for Higher Education Transformation

Gilligan C (1981) Moral development. In: Chickering & Associates (eds) *The Modern American College: Responding to the New Realities of Diverse Students and a Changing Society*. San Francisco: Jossey-Bass

Gilligan C (1982) *In a Different Voice: Psychological Theory and Women's Development*. Cambridge, MA: Harvard University Press

Glannon W (2005) *Biomedical Ethics*. Oxford: Oxford University Press

Grayson DJ (1996) A holistic approach to preparing disadvantaged students to succeed in tertiary science studies. Part I: Design of the Science Foundation programme (SFP). *International Journal of Science Education*, 18(8): 993–1013

Grayson DJ (1997) A holistic approach to preparing disadvantaged students to succeed in tertiary science studies. Part II: Outcomes of the Science Foundation programme (SFP). *International Journal of Science Education*, 19(1): 107–123

Grussendorff S, Liebenberg M and Houston J (2004) Selection for the Science Foundation Programme (University of Natal): The development of a selection instrument. *South African Journal of Higher Education*, 18(1): 265–272

Gunderson M (2005) Book review: Cultivating Humanity: A Classical Defense of Reform in Liberal Education. *The Interdisciplinary Journal of Study Abroad*, 11(1): 245–248

Gupta A (2006) *Affirmative action in higher education in India and the US: A study in contrasts*. Research and Occasional Paper Series: CSHE.10.06. Berkeley: University of California

Hall C, Juhila K, Parton N and Pösö T (2003) *Constructing Clienthood in Social Work and Human Services: Interaction, identities and practices.* London: Jessica Kingsley

Hamrick F, Evans N and Schuh J (2002) *Foundations of Student Affairs Practice: How Philosophy, Theory, and Research Strengthen Educational Outcomes.* San Francisco: Jossey-Bass

Harper A (1996) *Overview of departments of student services/affairs at South African institutions of higher education.* Education Policy Unit. Cape Town: University of the Western Cape

Health Professions Act, No. 56 of 1974 and Health Professions Amendment Act, No. 29 of 2007, Republic of South Africa

Health Professions Council of South Africa (HPCSA) (2008) Guidelines for good practice in the health care professions. In *National Patients' Rights Charter,* Booklet 3. Pretoria: HPCSA

Helen Suzman Foundation (2013) Focus. March. Available at http://www.bdlive.co.za/national/education/2013/student-financial-aid-scheme [accessed 3 April 2013]

Hirt J (2006) *Where You Work Matters: Student Affairs Administration at Different Types of Institutions.* Lanham: University Press of America

ISAP (2009) German responses to the latest developments in the Bologna Process: online. Available at http://www.iiepassport.org/germany [accessed 7 June 2010]

Jansen J (2012) Dear Jobless Graduate. *The Times*: 21 June 2012

Jennings L, Sovereign A, Bottorff N, Pederson-Mussel M and Vye C (2005) Nine Ethical Values of Master Therapists. *Journal of Medical Health Counselling*, 27(1): 32–47

Jones B, Coetzee G, Bailey T and Wickham S (2008) Factors that Facilitate Success for Disadvantaged Higher Education Students. Cape Town: Rural Education Access Programme (REAP). Available at http://www.reap.org.za/pieces/reports/pdf/tracking_reports/2008_June_factors_that_facilitate_success.pdf [accessed 24 February 2014]

Kania J and Kramer M (2011) Collective Impact. *Stanford Social Innovation Review*, Winter

Keeling RP (ed.) (2004) *Learning Reconsidered. A Campus-wide Focus on the Student Experience.* Washington DC: NASPA

Kessel AS (1998) Ethics and Research in Psychiatry. *International Review of Psychiatry*, 10: 331–337

Kezar A (2004) Obtaining integrity? Reviewing and examining the charter between higher education and society. *The Review of Higher Education,* 27(4): 429–459

Khoza R (2011) *Attuned Leadership – African Humanism as Compass.* Johannesburg: Penguin

King P and Baxter-Magolda M (1996) A developmental perspective on learning. *Journal of College Student Development*, 37(2): 163–173

Kirby NF (n.d.) Foundation Science Student Performance explained. Insight Gained at UKZN. Centre for Science Access, University of KwaZulu-Natal. Pietermaritzburg.

Kloot B, Case J and Marshall D (2008) A critical review of the educational philosophies underpinning science and engineering foundation programmes. *South African Journal of Higher Education*, 22(4): 799–816

Korten DC (1990) *Getting to the 21st Century: Voluntary Action and the Global Agenda.* West Hartford: Kumaria

Kretzman JP and McKnight JL (1993) *Building Communities from Inside Out.* Chicago: Acta

Kuh GD and Hu S (2001) The effects of student–faculty interaction in the 1990s. *Review of Higher Education*, 24(3): 309–332

Kuh G, Kinzie J, Schuh J and Whitt E (2010) *Student Success in College.* San Francisco: Jossey-Bass

Kuh G, Lyons J, Miller T and Trow J (1995) *Reasonable Expectations: Renewing the Educational Compact between Institutions and Students.* Washington DC: NASPA

Kuh G, Schuh J, Whitt E and Associates (1991) *Involving Colleges: Successful approaches to Fostering Student Learning and Development outside the Classroom.* San Francisco: Jossey-Bass

Lange L (2010) *Access and throughput in South African higher education: Three case studies.* Available at http://www.che.ac.za/documents/d000206/HigherEducationMonitor9.pdf [accessed 11 November 2011]

Letseka M, Breier M and Visser M (2010). Poverty, race and student achievement in seven higher education institutions. In: M Letseka, M Crosser, M Breier and M Visser (eds) *Student Retention and Graduate Destination: Higher Education and Labour Market Access and Success.* Cape Town: HSRC Press. pp25–40

Liu A, Rhoads R and Wang Y (2007) Chinese university students' views on globalization: Exploring conceptions of citizenship. *Chung Cheng Educational Studies*, 6(1): 95–125

Loeftstedt J and Shangwu Z (2002) China's transition patterns. In: H Daun (ed.) *Educational Restructuring in the Context of Globalization and National Policy.* New York: Routledge Falmer

Luckett K (2005) A critical policy analysis of the proposed National Quality Assurance System for South African Higher Education. In: M Smout (ed.) *The Decade Ahead: The Challenges for Quality Assurance in South African Higher Education.* Pretoria: South African Universities Vice-Chancellors Association

Ludeman R (2009) Report to HESA on student attrition in higher education in South Africa. Unpublished report presented in power-point format. HESA

Luescher-Mamashela T (2008) *Student governance in transition: University democratisation and managerialism.* PhD Dissertation. Cape Town: University of Cape Town

Lumadi TE and Mampuru KC (2010) Managing change in the student affairs divisions of higher education institutions. *South African Journal of Higher Education* 24(5): 716–729

Mabila T, Malatje S, Addo-Bediako A, Kazeni M and Mathabatha S (2006) The role of foundation programmes in science education: The UNIFY programme at the University of Limpopo, South Africa. *International Journal of Educational Development*, 26: 295–304

Madiba M (2009) *Investigating design issues in e-learning.* PhD dissertation. Cape Town: University of the Western Cape

Mail & Guardian (2012) Damning Report fails Motshega. 13 to 19 July

Mail & Guardian (2012) I was bribed, says N Cape hospital chief. 27 July to 2 August

Makwana M (2004) Leadership Challenges: A South African perspective. In: TNA Meyer & I Boninelli (eds) *Conversations in Leadership: South African Perspective. Randburg*: Knowledge Resources

Malina B (1988) Patron and client: The analogy behind the Synopsis Theology. *Forum* 4(1): 2–32

Mandew M (1993) Exploring the notion of 'cultural capital' and its implications for educational development. Proceedings of the 1993 Conference of the South African Association for Academic development, University of the Western Cape 1–3 December 1993

Mandew M (2003) *A Guide to Student Services in South Africa.* Pretoria: Centre for Higher Education Transformation

Mandela N (2010) *Conversations with Myself.* London: Macmillan

Mangcu X (2011) *Sobukwe.* City Press 3 April 2011

Manning J, Kinzie J and Schuh J (2006) *One Sze Does Not Fit All: Traditional and Innovative Models of Student Affairs Practice.* Oxford: Taylor & Francis

Masvawure TB (2008) 'I just need to be flashy on campus': Transactional Sex at an African University. Unpublished thesis, University of Pretoria

Maxwell JC, Graves SR and Addington TG (2005) *Life@Work – Marketplace success for people of faith.* Nashville: Thomas Nelson

Mayson C (1999) *Getting our act together to regenerate morality*, Mail & Guardian 6–12 September

Mbeki T (1998) *Africa: The Time Has Come: At the helm of South Africa's renaissance*, Inaugural address as chancellor of the University of Transkei, Umtata, 18 May 1995. Cape Town: Tafelberg

Mbigi L (1997) *The African Dream in Management.* Randburg: Knowledge Resources

McKnight j and Kretzman JP (1993) *Building Communities from Inside Out.* Chicago: ACTA

Meyer TNA and Boninelli I (2004) *Conversations in Leadership: A South African Perspective.* Randburg: Knowles Resources

Meilman PW and Pattis JA (1994) Suicide attempts and threats on college campus: Policy and Practice' *Journal of American College Health,* 42(4): 147–154

Merrick B. (2007) *Preparation for success: Key themes in the Prime Minister's initiative for international education* (UK). 2007 ISANA International Conference, Adelaide. Available at www.isana.org.au/files/isana07final00049.pdf [accessed 8 June 2010]

Miley KK, O'Melia M and Du Bois B (2001) *Generalist Social Work Practice: An Empowering Approach.* Boston: Allyn and Bacon

Moja T and Hayward FM (2005) The Changing Face of Redress in South African Higher Education (1990–2005), *Journal of Higher Education,* 5(1): 5–10

Mokwena K (1997) Empowerment as a tool for community health development. *Journal of Comprehensive Health* 8(2): 66–70

Morales, AT and Sheafor BW (2004) *Social Work: A Profession with Many Faces 10th edn.* Boston: Pearson Education

Morreim EH (1993) Am I my brother's warden? Responding to the unethical or incompetent colleague. *The Hastings Centre Report,* 23(3): 19–27

Moulder J (1991) Remedial education programmes: Miracle or failure? *South African Journal of Higher Education,* 5(1): 5–10

Mphahlele MK (1994) Access, equity and redress in science academic development programmes: critical issues and concerns. In: S Levy (ed.) *Projects Speak for Themselves: Science and Maths Education in the Transition.* Pietermaritzburg: Shuter and Shooter

Mphahlele E (2004) ES'KIA CONTINUED. I am Because We Are 'Baccalaureate Address'. University of Pennsylvania, 16 May 1982. Johannesburg: Stainbank and Associates

National Planning Commission. (2011). National Development Plan. Vision for 2030. Pretoria: Government Printers

Nolte M (2010) *Student Support at the University of Pretoria.* SAASSAP Conference. NMMU. Port Elizabeth. October

Nuss E (2003) The development of student affairs. In: S Komives, D Woodard & Associates (eds) *Student Services: A handbook for the profession* (4th edn). San Francisco: Jossey-Bass

Nussbaum M (1995) Human capabilities, female human beings. In: M Nussbaum & J Glover (eds) *Women, Culture and Development. A Study of Human Capabilities.* Oxford: Clarendon Press

Pascarella E and Terenzini P (2005) *How College Affects Students: A third decade of research* (Vol. 2). San Francisco: Jossey-Bass

Parkin G (2004) E-Learning Adventures Beyond the LMS. Blogspot

Payne M (1997a) Routes to and through clienthood and their implications for practice. Available online at www.researchgate.net

Payne M (1997b) *Modern Social Work Theory.* Chicago: Lyceum Books

Payne RK, DeVol PE and Smith TD (2001) *Bridges out of Poverty: Strategies for Professionals and Communities.* Highlands, Texas: Aha!Process

Pence G (2000) *A Dictionary of Common Philosophical Terms.* Birmingham: McGraw Hill

Perry WG (1970) *Forms of Intellectual and Ethical Development in the College Years: A scheme.* New York: Holt, Rinehart and Winston

Pillay AL, Wassenaar DR and Kramers AL (2004) Attendance at psychological consultations following non-fatal suicidal behaviour: An ethical dilemma. *South African Journal of Psychology,* 34 (3): 350–363

Quiang Z (2003) Internationalization of higher education: Towards a conceptual framework. *Policy Future in Education,* 1(2): 248–269

Rachels J (2003) *The Elements of Moral Philosophy. New York:* McGraw Hill
Republic of South Africa (1997) Higher Education Act No. 107
Republic of South Africa (2002) Mental Health Care Act No. 17
Republic of South Africa (1978) Social Services Professions Act 110
Roberson MD and Walter G (2008) Many faces of the dual role dilemma in psychiatric ethics. *Australian and New Zealand Journal of Psychiatry*, 42: 228–235
South African Association of Counselling and Development in Higher Education (SAACDHE) (2007) *Position paper: Student counselling*. Paper presented by the national executive at the SAACDHE national executive meeting, Bloemfontein, 2007
Sandeen A and Barr MJ (2006) *Critical Issues for Student Affairs: Challenges and Opportunities*. San Francisco: Jossey-Bass
Schuh J (2003) *Contemporary Financial Issues in Student Affairs: New directions for Student Services*. San Francisco: Jossey-Bass
Scott I, Yeld N and Hendry J (2007) *Higher Education Monitor 6: A Case for Improving Learning and Teaching in South African Higher Education*. Pretoria: Council on Higher Education
Sen AK (1995) Gender inequality and theories of justice. In: M Nussbaum & J Glover (eds) *Women, Culture and Development. A study of human capabilities*. Oxford: Clarendon Press
Sen AK (2001) *Development as Freedom*. Oxford: Oxford University Press
Sheafor BW and Horejsi CJ (2011) *Techniques and Guidelines for Social Work Practice* (9th edn). Canada: Pearson
Sidhu R (2006) *Universities and Globalization: To Market, to Market*. Mahwah, NJ: Lawrence Erlbaum Associates
Singh M, Kenway J and Apple M (2005) Globalizing education: Perspectives from above and below. In: M Apple, J Kenway & M Singh (eds) *Globalizing Education*. New York: Peter Lang
Skidmore RA, Thackery MG and Farley OW (1991) *Introduction to Social Work* (5th edn). Englewood Cliffs: Prentice Hall
Speckman M (2006) Pearls hidden in poverty: A reflection on the plight of disadvantaged students at higher learning institutions. Paper presented at the SAASSAP Conference, University of the Free State, Bloemfontein, September
Speckman M (2007) *A Vision for Africa's Development?* Pietermaritzburg: Cluster
Speckman M (2009) A presentation at a function to thank Mr Louis von Zeuner. CEO of Absa for the contribution made to advance the Foundation Programmes offered at the Mamelodi campus of the University of Pretoria. The occasion recognised in particular the bursaries given to students from disadvantaged backgrounds. University of Pretoria, Mamelodi, October
Speckman M (2011) Presentation prepared for the UP Senior Management Beraad. Pretoria West, January
Stefani L (2011) Evaluating Academic Practice. In: L Stefani (ed.) *Evaluating the Effectiveness of Academic Development: Principles and Practice*. New York: Routledge
Strayhorn T (2006) Frameworks for assessing learning and development outcomes. Council for the Advancement of Standards in Higher Education. Washington DC: Library of Congress Cataloguing-in-Publication Data
Strode A, Slack C and Essack Z (2010) Child consent in South African Law: Implications for researchers, service providers and policy-makers. *South African Medical Journal*, 100(4): 247–249
Tabane OJJ, Bonakele T, Mxenge T and Thabakgale S (2003) *Student Representative Councils: A Guide to Developing a Constitution*. Cape Town: Centre for Higher Education Transformation

Thornton M, Bricheno P, Green R, Wankhede G, Iyer P and Reid I (2010) Diversity, Isolation and Integration in Higher Education: Intentions vs Experience. Paper presented at the Australian Association for Research in Education (AARE) 2010 International Education Research Conference, Melbourne, Australia. Available at http://ocs.sfu.ca/aare/index.php/AARE/AARE_2010/paper/view/1764 [accessed 12 August 2012]

Tinto V (1997) Classrooms as communities: Exploring the educational character of student persistence. *The Journal of Higher Education*, 68(6): 599–623

Tinto V (2008) Access without success is no opportunity. Keynote address. National Institute for Staff and Organisational Development. University of Texas, 26 May 2008

Tinto V (2012) Enhancing student success: Taking the classroom success seriously. *The International Journal of the First Year in Higher Education*, 3(1): 1–8. DOI: 10.5204/intjfyhe.v2i1.119

Trainor R (2002) *Student Services*. Universities UK, SCOP

Tyson DR (2010) Examining the Impact of the Humanities Access Programme 2001–2004: Throughput Rates and Students' Perceptions of the Programme. MA dissertation, Education in the Centre for Higher Education Studies, School of Education and Development, Faculty of Education, University of KwaZulu-Natal

UKCISA (1999) UK Prime Ministers Initiative (PMI). Available at http://www.ukcisa.org.uk/pmi/ [accessed 10 August 2012]

United Nations Educational, Scientific and Cultural Organization (UNESCO) (1998) *World Declaration on Higher Education for the Twenty-first Century*, adopted by the World Conference on Higher Education: Vision and Action, October 1998. Available at http://www.unesco.org/education/educprog/wche/declaration_eng.htm [accessed 17 June 2010]

United Nations Educational, Scientific and Cultural Organization (UNESCO) (2002) *The Role of Student Affairs and Services in Higher Education*. Paris: UNESCO

United States Department of Education (USDE) (2006) A test of leadership: Charting the future of U.S. higher education. A report of the commission appointed by Secretary of Education Margaret Spellings, September 2006. Available at http://www2.ed.gov/about/bdscomm/list/hiedfuture/reports/pre-pub-report.pdf [accessed 8 June 2010]

Urbanski M (2009) Special report: The Bologna Process: High hopes, frustrated students. Available at www.trinitynews.ie [accessed 7 June 2010]

Van der Berg S (2013) Beyond expectations: Progress of poor students through university. *Focus* 68: 6–12

Van der Flier H, Thijs G and Zaaiman H (2003) Selecting students for a South African mathematics and science foundation programme: The effectiveness and fairness of school-leaving examinations and aptitude tests. *International Journal of Educational Development*, 23: 399–409

Veyne P (1990) *Bread and Circuses: Historical Sociology and Political Pluralism*. London: Penguin

Volbrecht T and Boughey C (2004) Curriculum responsiveness from the margins? A reappraisal of academic development in South Africa. In: H Griesel (Ed.) *Curriculum Responsiveness: Case Studies in Higher Education*. Pretoria: SAUVCA

Waghid Y (2010) Re-imagining higher education in South Africa: On critical democratic education. *South African Journal of Higher Education* 24(4): 491–494

Waghid Y (2011) Education and hope: Stellenbosch University in the 21st century. *South African Journal of Higher Education* 25(1): 5–13

Wagner W (1996) *The Social Change Model of Leadership: A brief Overview*. College Park: National Clearinghouse for Leadership Programs.

Walker M and Badsha N (1993) Academic development: The 1990s. *South African Journal of Higher Education*, 7(1): 59–62

Wang H (2004). Emerging student services in China. *Student Affairs Newsletter: Facilitating Student Success*, 9–11. Fullerton: California State University

Weidman J (1989) Undergraduate socialization: A conceptual approach. In: J Smart (ed.) *Higher Education: A handbook of Theory and Research, 5*. New York: Agathon

West C (2006) Nelson Mandela: Great exemplar of the grand democratic tradition. In: X Mangcu. (ed.) *The Meaning of Mandela: A Literary and Intellectual Celebration*. Johannesburg: Human Sciences Research Council

Wharton, L (n.d.) *Moral Leadership: A Pipedream*. Available at www.leader-values.com/Content/detail [accessed 23 July 2012]

Winte, B (1994) *Seek the Welfare of the City: Christians as Benefactors and Citizens*. Michigan: Eerdmans

Wood L and Lithauer P (2005) The 'added value' of a foundation programme. *South African Journal*, 19(5)

Za'rour GI (1988) Universities in Arab countries. Population and Human Resource Department, World Bank: The International Bank for Development and Reconstruction. Available at http://books.google.co.za/books?hl=en&lr=&id=nh-C1 [accessed 17 December 2009]

www.ingramcontent.com/pod-product-compliance
Lightning Source LLC
Chambersburg PA
CBHW071411300426
44114CB00016B/2265